Spiritual
Detox
for
Divas

Two Girls Gossip about Relationships,
Soul Contracts, Cord-Cutting,
Manifesting, and More

Amy R Brooks
& Jennifer Jiva

Spiritual Detox for Divas
© 2016
VoicePenPurpose Publishing ™

Published December 12, 2016
ISBN: 978-0-9978394-3-2

DISCLAIMER

-Dedication-

For all the Divas who need to remember what they already know and who they have always been.

Table of Contents

(Super Important) Introduction..1

Chapter 1: Who are You?..9

Chapter 2: Past Lives and Soul Contracts 19

Chapter 3: Cord Cutting..49

Chapter 4: Chakras & Crystals...63

Chapter 5: Card Reading 85

Chapter 6: Deceased Loved Ones & Spirit Guides 99

Chapter 7: Synchronicity...109

Chapter 8: Meditation & Mindfulness 125

Chapter 9: Intuition 137

Chapter 10: Supporting Energy in Relationships..........145

Chapter 11: Manifesting Stuff...163

Chapter 12: Connections to Everything 173

Afterword...183

About the Authors..189

(Super Important)
Introduction

You picked up this book because you're curious, but you're not quite sure what to expect. First question: What *is* a Spiritual Detox? Will gross drinks be involved? According to us, a Spiritual Detox is the process of getting rid of things that don't make sense in your life and getting your spiritual power back. This book is for ladies who are sick of the way things have been in their lives. You may not be drawn to every aspect of this book, but we can almost guarantee that there will be nuggets of information that will make all the difference in your life.

We recognize that the spiritual, woo woo books you normally see don't necessarily appeal to you. You feel like they're written for someone who already knows all the fundamental information about this subject matter. You, friend, are open to new ideas, but are not willing to believe everything someone tells you just because they say it with authority.

Perfect!

Now to the Diva aspect of this book. The dictionary defines a diva in negative terms. That's bananas. We're taking the word back. *We* define a "Diva" as a discerning woman who doesn't listen to bullshit and thinks for herself. She stands up boldly in this world, instead of sitting politely. Divas are leaders. Divas are Earth goddesses. Divas stay in their pajamas with a messy bun until noon. Divas rock stiletto heels. Divas start their own businesses. Divas are amazing mothers. Divas are sexy singles. Divas are the best girlfriends you could hope for. Divas are whatever and whoever they want to be.

This book is just for Divas. If you're reading this, you're exactly where you're supposed to be at this point in your life. The ladies who pick up this book are the exact type of Divas who will find comfort and confirmation on a deep level by reading about new things that stretch their understanding. Divas are curious and seek understanding.

The reason why we are writing this book was because women were asking us great questions about life, meaning, and connection. We decided to let you in on our conversation about the basics since that's where understanding is created; with the basics.

There will be times when we talk about ideas that seem strange or even silly, but on some level most of the concepts will resonate with you. You know, because you're a Diva! Even if the language or exercises seem far out, the meaning behind them will make sense to you. On a soul-level you will "remember" your connection to everyone and everything. Divas get it: the bigger picture is more important than a momentary feeling of separation or confusion.

Talking about a Soul Detox means talking a lot about energy. To view this in broader terms, every major religion and field of science speak to energy and the power of energy exchange. Religions call this energetic phenomenon love, miracles, or grace. Scientists refer to it as combustion, attraction, or kinetic energy. Regardless, energy is everywhere and can defy the separation and distance that limits our usual sense of physical reality.

What?!

Let's say that in a different way:

Energy can go everywhere, and doesn't understand distance. Every single thing is energy, the same energy. It doesn't matter if you're talking about a human or wild hog. You and a wild hog are both composed of energy; even if you're super smart and can text a friend and a hog can't. In the end, you're both still made up of energy.

Taking that even further, energy exists even in things we cannot see. We're all connected to *everything*. Here's one of the most important lessons in this book (spoiler alert): There is no need to put limitations on things that are tangible or touchable. Life, and energy, are full of surprises.

We'll explain more later, but at this point it's important to understand that this book is going to ask you to be open to a broader perspective. You hereby have permission to be open-minded. Say to yourself, "I'm going to open myself up to the possibility to connect with everything." And when you mentally and emotionally open yourself up, you will start to feel the shift. If you are open on a soulful level, you will even be able to get past the literal world and the need for extensive proof to justify everything.

Warning: some Divas may have felt triggered or irritated because we glossed over your need for "extensive proof," but we can't linger on this need for proof for too long. We know that you may feel uncomfortable with various ideas ahead, but we have to keep going and hope for the best. We love you, Divas, but any reassurance you may need will come in the chapters ahead, not in this introduction.

If trusting us feels scary, that's cool! Most new things (and people) are scary at first. One way to overcome your default fear is to just start saying "yes" to things that feel good (and aren't dangerous or hurting anyone) and don't stop to worry about all the things that *could* go wrong.

As you read this book, we want you to start saying, "yes" to a new understanding. Saying "yes" opens you up to a different way of experiencing your human existence. On the flip side, saying "no" shuts your energy down. Think of it like someone is knocking at your door (don't overanalyze the situation and peep nervously through the hole) allow the new person, or in this case, the experiences, into your life.

We also know that you are going to respond to this book based on your past belief system. Everyone has had different experiences with religion and all of that history will influence how you interpret the topics in this book. Quick example: if you say *angels* to Catholics they will welcome those stories, but others may be turned off. Just know that some of your reactions will be directly connected to your religious norms. It's all a-okay.

Recently Jennifer got into a conversation with her friend about the power of a full moon. "I believe in God, not the moon," the friend declared.

She responded, "I get what you're saying, but what if God created the moon as a guide for us; to help us understand cycles?"

In that moment she decided not to identify which belief was real or better; she didn't choose between God or the moon. In the end, she was suggesting all of these seemingly contradictory ideas come from the same place.

Even though contradictory ideas show up in our religion, more and more people are opening up to the idea that Jesus, Muhammad, and Buddha conveyed the same message with different faces. To that end, this book can speak to you no matter what faith tradition you embrace. Regardless of your specific beliefs, Divas understand that we are all one and come from the same place. No matter what, we are all connected and can learn from one another.

There's a lot to learn from topics in this book that may seem new and strange. As far as specific content, this book will be an introduction to encounters with angels, contacting deceased lost loved ones, cutting cords, and rewriting soul contracts among other things. They will all be discussed in a safe, loving way. Please know that there are ways to look at the topics we are covering through your own lens, but you are encouraged try to view them with a clean perspective as well.

We will offer answers that may seem to come from outside of your past beliefs. We know that if you are looking for answers, this book may influence your opinions, but it will resonate with everyone differently. At this point, just try to open up to the inner dialogue and see how you *feel* as you read and contemplate the new information.

Since the format of this book is a conversation, we hope that you will feel like you're just hanging out with two gals simply gossiping about spiritual stuff. Take the nuggets that appeal to you and feel free to ignore us (for now) if a particular topic feels like too much of a stretch. **In the end, we are not trying to push ideas on anyone; we are just having a conversation and inviting you to listen in.**

Another structural note: there will be lots of tools offered and an optional homework assignment at the end of each chapter. The way you interpret and use each tool during your homework is up to you. There are so many ways to implement the lessons we cover! At the very least, we hope you enjoy our conversations about the specifics of spiritual connection and how energy impacts *everything*.

We wrote this book because we knew that if we got to talking about the ins and outs of mystical practice, a lot of people could connect with the spiritual world on a more intimate level. Hopefully this (super important) introduction makes you feel more comfortable eavesdropping on the conversation that's about to start.

Remember: You deserve to feel a human *and* spiritual belonging while you're on this big Earth. It's time to discuss *how* that's possible!

Hugs,
Amy and Jennifer

A Spiritual Detox

is a cleansing of the soul

and

a reminder to the heart that

YOU *have all the power.*

CHAPTER 1

Who are You?

Amy: Hello, sweet Jennifer!

Jennifer: Hey, love muffin! I'm ridiculously excited that we're doing this!

Amy: Me, too! It feels good to actually discuss these topics in an organized and purposeful way.

Jennifer: I know...we've been talking about a need for a book like this, but I'm still beyond thrilled that we're actually doing it! And I love that it's for Divas!

Amy: Me, too! To *everything* you just said. So let's get started! First, we should talk about who we are before we get into the deep stuff.

Jennifer: Good idea. You go first.

Amy: Okay. I'm a writer and book coach. I love working with first-time authors to help them take their book idea from concept to reality. I started VoicePenPurpose Publishing ™ so that everyone could have easy access to writing coaches, ghostwriters, formatters, graphic designers, web designers, etc. The goal is help folks share their story in a polished and permanent way. I love it so much!

Jennifer: It's your purpose. You're living on purpose, girl!

Amy: I agree. I'm so happy. I used to teach English in high school and then I tried middle school for a little while. After being in the classroom for 16 years, I decided to resign and shift my focus to working with adults. It's a really fun way to use my love of writing and working with "students" in a different way.

Jennifer: Oh, I love it so much! At some point you're going to need to tell everyone the story of how you and I met and what happened that led to your new life.

Amy: You mean our first conversation that changed the trajectory of my entire existence?

Jennifer: Ha! Yep. I still remember that day very clearly.

Amy: I'll definitely find a way to bring that up later, but for now, let's meet you.

Jennifer: Okay, okay. I know I'm all over the place. That's why I need you. Keep me focused, momma!

Amy: So you're an intuitive guide, some would call you a psychic. Is that a title you use? Oh...*and* you're an energy healer?

Jennifer: Yes, I use both those titles. But it is interesting because it sometimes depends on who's asking. I work a lot with women online who ask, "What do you do?" When I first came into the "online" world, I was actually focusing on business coaching, coaching people who run their own businesses. And then I realized that I don't ever want to box myself in or labeling myself as a business coach. It was a good field because it's full of people who need to hear that they have a specific purpose, and questions about what that is, but I don't want to limit myself to that. That's why this book is good; it's for *all* the Divas out there.

Amy: So you think this book will clear things up for people who have limited understanding of psychic stuff *and* will help them understand what you actually do?

Jennifer: Oh, definitely! Let's see if I can answer your previous question a little better, at least in regard to what I "do" and my role with this book.

I feel like this book is being channeled through me. I'm just here to facilitate a message that so many people need to hear. In this book I am delivering information so women can learn how to live their best life, understand what their truth is, and find healing.

In general, people need to know that information comes *through* me and can help others in ways that I don't even realize. I had a woman recently tell me how everything has shifted in her life because of me and our sessions together. That's great, but until she told me that, I had no idea. Sometimes I go comatose and don't even remember what I said. I like the idea of being called an intuitive healer more than psychic. That descriptor feels right.

Amy: What does your family think about all of the intuitive and energy work you do?

Jennifer: Oh, my gosh! I was *not* raised with this open, you know, free-thinking outlook. Actually, my parents were the polar opposite; we never had the open conversations that I have now with my kids. My mom is super logical. That being said, we weren't raised with a particular religion. Actually, the only time I went to church growing up was by myself or with my friends. It turns out my dad was Jehovah's Witness, but never discussed it with us. I only found out when I was sixteen and he passed away. I inherited his Jehovah's Witness Bible which shocked me. I then made the connection that maybe that's why he refused treatment for his cancer. Religion aside and back to my family today, my mom has only recently started to open up to what I do.

Amy: Really? I didn't realize that.

Jennifer: It's true. For example, not too long ago my mom broke her ankle in three places. She had to have surgery and plates put in to repair everything. She stayed with my aunt for seven weeks as she healed. During her recovery, I went over to do energy work on her. My mom ended up not needing any prescription pain medication. Even though she had a huge cast on, I could still work on her. That's the beauty of energy work, it doesn't matter what the physical circumstances are, like a heavy cast; it is still effective. It even works when you're not together. Most of my clients live very far away from me, actually.

Amy: Wow. It's kind of incredible that you're just getting to this place with your mom. I mean, you've known her your whole life, but you're just now connecting on this deeper level.

Jennifer: I know. She wasn't really down with spiritual stuff either. She couldn't even pronounce the word "reiki" when I began getting my certifications, but then she began to become more open after I worked on her personally and she learned more about energy work. And it's not just shifting with my mom, either. My aunt, the one she had stayed with, has had hip pain forever. While I was visiting my mom, I decided to do some energy work on my aunt, too.

Side-note: my aunt had someone say to her, "don't you dare let her do that to you" before I started. She told my aunt that she could get "bad stuff" from someone else that I may have worked on in the past. I hear that sometimes; people worry that I'm calling in bad energy or spreading energy from one person to another.

Amy: Is that a valid concern?

Jennifer: Not with me, but energy work is a hard thing to explain. I always ask my guides for simple ways to explain how all this works. Recently it was shown to me to compare energy work to sex.

Ha! It *is* like sex. Unprotected sex.

Amy: Really? I need more explanation on this one.

Jennifer: It's hilarious, but it's true! Before sex with a new person, you need to ask, "Who is this person? What do I know about them?" It's the same with an energy worker. In either case, go out on a date (so to speak) and get to know them before you open up your energies.

With an intuitive or energy worker, you should take time to have a call first, check how you feel after connecting with them, follow them on social media, see if you feel any hesitancy. If you're nervous about working with them, ask yourself why. Am I receiving a warning from my subconscious? Is this a genuine concern? If you don't have any second-thoughts about opening up to them and you feel good, take the next step. Definitely trust your inner voice; it's got your best interest at heart.

Amy: Working with an energy healer is like unprotected sex. Hmmm, that makes me feel icky.

Jennifer: I know! But it's kind of a big deal. I squirm when I see people casually entering into energy work. I want to tell all Divas: Be careful who you open yourself up to!

Amy: Hmmmm. I'm starting to get the comparison and it makes me wonder if someone reading this is thinking about how they opened themselves up to sex without realizing the impact of that energy exchange.

Jennifer: Oh, I know. Just remember: everyone you have sex with stays with you energetically. They stay stuck with you in your energy field. You have to shed any negative forces that were once welcome from that exchange. Which is still true with all human interactions, actually.

Amy: I see what you're saying. All physically and spiritually intimate relationships should require some getting to know one another first. I see people jump into very intimate relationships with psychics, intuitives, card/palm readers that they do not know *at all* and it feels pretty risky.

Oh, just like sleeping around or a one-night stand! I understand your analogy even more now than I did at first. You're saying we should take some time to get to know anyone *first* before we open our whole-self up to that level of energy exchange.

Jennifer: Exactly! Just take it slow and make sure you have a good feeling about the interaction *before* you start working together.

Amy: What homework could readers do if they want to clear some of their past energy connections? From a sexual encounter or a bad experience with an energy worker.

Jennifer: We are going to get into those action steps some more when we talk about soul contracts and cord-cutting. How about for now we start off slow and make some lists?

Amy: Sounds good to me, I love making lists!

Homework:

Think of exchanges (sexual or not) that made you wish you could go back in time and avoid that person or situation. Make a list of names/situations. Next to each one, reflect on how well you got to know the person before you entered into that particular relationship and mixed your energy with theirs.

CHAPTER 2

Past Lives and Soul Contracts

Amy: What do we need to know about past lives? From what I understand, the idea is that our souls do not cease to exist when we die; instead they can inhabit new human forms if they choose. Why is this important to understand?

Jennifer: This topic is fascinating to me! I heard something interesting about birthmarks a little while ago: I read in an article about how birthmarks can indicate how you passed on in a past life based on where the mark is on your body. For example, if you had a birthmark on your stomach you may have suffered a traumatic wound there or something internally that ended your life.

Something resonated so deeply with me about it, that I became borderline obsessed with learning more about past lives and how they could impact your current life. I came across an intriguing article about kids who were talking about their past lives. They were young and innocent and talking about who they *used* to be. To me our children are our greatest source of information when it comes to these subjects.

For example, one boy told his parents he remembered that he was a woman who had jumped out of a window during a fire. The parents did a little research using details he told them and they found old photos of the deadly fire he had described. They lined all the photos up they found in front of him and asked him what he thought. As soon as he saw the photos, he identified himself as Nicky, one of the women in the photos. His soul remembered and recognized the past life. The parents weren't necessarily into woo woo stuff, but they really listened to their son and were convinced that there was no way he could have known about the fire if he hadn't been there. It gives me goose-bumps just recalling it.

Amy: That's creepy-cool. If I'm being honest, it would scare me a little to hear one of my three boys talking about their past lives. I try never to be dismissive, though. I hope I could be as loving as the parents you just described.

Jennifer: I agree so much. When we really stay present, and listen, really listen we can allow others to go deeper. It's so important to hold the space and actually let people share their truth without judgement or criticism.

Shortly after reading about that little boy, I found myself in a spiritual class in which one of the exercises was to lead adult women through their past lives and the healing that can come from revisiting them. It's important to remember that we come with a cellular memory that contains every life we have ever lived and stays with us through our current incarnation. Traumas, belief systems, fears, attachments, etcetera can also come from previous lives. This is why we start our lives with certain dispositions.

Amy: I have often wondered if some souls are older than others and can offer insights that seem out of place considering their physical age.

Jennifer: I'm so interested in this, what do you mean? Explain more.

Amy: Well, when it comes to wisdom, I think our physical age may be less significant that our soul's age. I think about children who we label as "old souls." Obviously, they are still kids, but a lot of adults see something different shine through that makes them seem older or wiser at times. My eldest son has had this identity assigned to him by countless adults from the day they met him. He seems to get things on a soul level that is surprising if you consider his age.

Jennifer: I have thought more of the *experience* of our souls versus actual age. What has you pondering this?

Amy: Funny you ask! Sometimes I have visions or insights when I drive alone or when I'm in the shower...

Jennifer: Sounds about right!

Amy: So the other day, while I was rolling solo in the car, I had a really clear vision of me arguing with someone who was "Earth older" than me and he was talking down to me. In a moment of frustration, I said, "look, my soul is older than yours, so there are some things you won't understand."

I don't really know where that came from and I wanted to see what you thought.

Jennifer: Ohhhhhhh! That vision fascinates me!

Amy: And that brings us back to folks who are considered "old souls" or children/teens who seem wise beyond their years.

Jennifer: It makes perfect sense. Through their experiences in each life they have gained knowledge and wisdom. I've been really aware of this idea since I recently turned 40. I had so many people asking me how I felt about this significant milestone as if I were "old" now. To each person I expressed how proud I am to be 40. The knowledge and wisdom from this current life alone has been so significant and life changing. It has given me the opportunity to help so many. I think the reason I am brought to this example is to help others compare what each of us must feel when we enter a new incarnation. There is so much growth we will experience and so much help we can offer.

Amy: And we can apply this to the subconscious memories we have from those past lives?

Jennifer: Yep. When I witnessed this in sessions with my clients, they would end up in their past life and discover the important people in their life and death. While looking at their past life, they would discover what their talents were in that life, as well as any struggles they had. They sometimes recognized family members from that life that are family members in this life. They saw fears they had, love they shared. There are so many amazing things to be gained from past life work. In the end, people say, "Oh that makes so much sense!" On some level, they recognized how those roles play out in their current life or how current patterns, beliefs, or interests become even clearer.

I had a past life regression 10 years ago and at the time I had crazy paranoia about my youngest son Jackson. At the time, I'd always have to keep Jackson right next to me in the bedroom, pool; everywhere. If he wasn't within my sight, I'd get really nervous and upset. I also had an awareness of how I would get particularly stressed when we were around water. That was when my anxiety was the highest. When I did the regression, I learned that in a life I lived in the 1800s I had son named Jack who had drowned when he was 4. I was bawling through this entire process; the memory was so painful, as if it were happening all over. Energetically, of course, it was.

After revisiting this life, I was able to calm myself to a certain extent because I had an explanation of my fear. However, I couldn't move on completely because those paranoid tapes still played in my head, the volume was just turned down a couple of notches. It then occurred to me that although I had awareness, I had no healing.

Fortunately, I recognized this and revisited this life once more and did healing work this time. I was then able to get a handle on those irrational fears and give Jackson the space and freedom to be the Jackson this life called for. Which is good, because Jackson is a really carefree kid. If he had a fearful mother hovering over him all the time, he wouldn't be able to live his best life with the freedom that he needs.

Now I understand that people can work through their past life experiences and heal the pain in *this* life. We can do the healing now. It's a passion of mine to help people heal from the hurt they've been carrying around in this life *and* past ones. This is important so that everyone we are connected to can live a freer life, too. Past pain can cause a domino effect and impact a lot of people.

Healing the past has the potential to change everyone's future in a positive way and who doesn't want that?

Amy: That's really moving. I now feel more urgency to address this in my own lifetime; for everyone's sake. What else have you learned about yourself from your past lives?

Jennifer: It's funny; in the past I had always had trouble accepting money in exchange for my intuitive and healing gifts. It turned out in many past lives I was ridiculed, threatened, and even put to death for being a witch or magical. I know that is why I had hesitation in the past around allowing people to show gratitude for my work with payment when there was so much shame and fear around it for me in previous lives.

I also discovered that I lived many lives as a member of the clergy and I loved serving as a monk. Obviously that is a very charitable existence, and I don't want to lose those qualities. Plus, I love being of service and helping people now. I choose to keep that trait, but without exhausting myself. Money is not the only thing exchanged, there is also an energy exchange. It must be an equal energy exchange. What I mean by that, is you should not go out of your way to help someone over and over only if there is never (or very seldom) anything coming back in return to assist you from that person. That is not an even energy exchange and should not be tolerated. It is not respecting yourself.

I used to have a hard time asking for anything in return for my efforts, even like emotional or energetic support. I was offering it out, but not allowing it to come back to me. I've since learned from my past lives that I don't have to always be of service without reciprocation.

Until I really needed support recently, I didn't realize how rarely I allowed myself to accept help. Now that I know this about my past, I can recognize it in my daily life and chose to be open to reciprocal energy exchange.

People can look at their current behaviors that may be left over from a past life and reflect on how those traits to show up in this life. They can decide which ones they want to keep and which ones they want to release. This is advised to be done with assistance of a skilled professional or healer that you resonate with and trust.

Not everything that comes from the past is bad. I really feel the need to emphasize that. Many talents can be brought forward from past lives. Understanding of family relationships and dynamics and how they are woven through time in different roles really offers up understanding in ways nothing else would allow.

Amy: I like the idea that you can learn from past lives and build on them to be more fully actualized in this lifetime.

Jennifer: Exactly! Look at you; you have several past lives of being writers who didn't finish their books. You were really bothered by that, so you worked your butt off to finish your first book.

Amy: I know! I remember when I first heard that about myself; my *past* self. You did a quick reading for me where you told me about the secrecy and frustration that surrounded my writing and the publishing of my ideas. In that moment, I got super determined to just finish my book so I would make my soul happy. Later, when it was in my hands, I felt like, "We finally did it, soul! It's official; no more carrying around the pain of unfulfilled destiny."

Now I tell everyone: once you're a published author, you'll always be a published author. A weight, that I don't completely understand, was lifted. Done and done.

Jennifer: Ha, I love it! That reminds me of another woman I worked with who had problems conceiving. In her past life she was a male (this is true for a lot of women who lack maternal instinct or have trouble conceiving in this life) who, in the past life, lost his love and his baby. That pain was so deep and on some level her soul equated pregnancy with that feeling of pain and loss.

Amy: What was her reaction to that information from your session together?

Jennifer: She immediately said, "Wow, that totally resonates with me. I know that to be true." She was previously confused why she couldn't conceive. 13 years of trying to have a baby and now she had some sense of peace about it. She knew it to be true pain that her soul had experienced in another life.

Amy: Can you explain how our past life roles show up in this life?

Jennifer: Definitely! Parenting roles are particularly interesting. My oldest son has always resisted me as an authority figure; basically he doesn't see me as his mom. He is in his twenties now and has even said as an adult, "I'm so sorry that I didn't let you parent me more as a child." That was amazing to hear because he was *so* difficult at times. He has always been strongly opinionated about my life and he sometimes acts like he's *my* parent. I never understood why he seemed so invested in my decision-making. I now realize that in a past life we played different roles in our family and he was in a parenting role. In fact, he recently said to me when we talked about this that, he always felt more like my father.

Amy: I bet there are a lot of people who have a dynamic like that in their family. I've heard people describe their relationship with a parent as if they, even as a child, always felt like the older, wiser one who had to watch over that particular adult.

Jennifer: Interestingly, our roles in past lives often impact the relationship to our mother figure. I'm not sure why, but it mostly comes up with someone's relationship to the maternal role. There are shifts so that a soul might be a child in one lifetime and then switch roles with the mother in the next lifetime.

All of these role changes can trigger old patterns of hurt between people that can become residual and carried from one life to another. Carrying things with you from one life to the next can obviously cause conflict. Souls who have constant struggle or leftover "stuff" often choose to process it by coming back as siblings. In fact, a lot of people stay in the same "soul family" because they contract to stay together through different lives and play different roles to support and help one another grow.

Amy: So you're saying that our souls sometimes choose to come back as siblings to hash out old differences? That kind of blows my mind, but I can see how sibling conflicts could be a safe place to resolve issues.

Jennifer: I know! The way it has been shown to me is that most siblings live under the same roof as children and have that day in and day out interaction and they don't have the option to just choose to leave. If they had chosen to come back as friends or lovers, they may bow out because it is much easier to do and because they can.

It's also lovely and interesting that people also choose to incarnate as soul mates: friends or lovers, and they have that instant "knowing" that they've met them before when they first reconnect on Earth. It's immediate. It's a soul recognition.

Some people instantly "see" that connection and celebrate it, while other people get freaked out and avoid those relationships because they feel too intense or uncomfortably familiar.

Amy: I have experienced many relationships like that. I *love* it. Soul lives overlapping is just about the most miraculous thing I can imagine.

Kind of related to that idea, what do you think of grandparents dying right before a baby in the family is born?

Jennifer: Oh! I call it "the changing of the guards" when that happens. Sometimes people can come back quickly and the baby embodies that particular person who just passed or it could be someone else from that soul family. When one person leaves this existence, another person appears.

I've seen it in my own lifetime. I became pregnant with my first child at 17. My dad died when I was 16, only a little over a year earlier. When I turned 18, my son was born on my birthday (our exact birth times are only 16 minutes apart). Even though I knew I was young, I never wavered in my decision to have him. Everybody wanted me to get an abortion or give the baby up for adoption. Those never felt like options to me.

Somehow I knew he was going to be a boy and I had his name picked out way in advance. Brendan was born on his due date- which is super rare, by the way, only 5% of babies arrive on their due date!

And I knew on some level- though I didn't consciously think it- that if my dad had to leave, Brendan was the gift he gave me to help me get through the pain. From the beginning Brendan's energy was very much like "you are not in charge of me." Like I said before, it was hard for him to accept me in the role of his mother. He openly acknowledges that dynamic now that he's an adult and can see how our soul contract has played out during this lifetime.

My pregnancy 10 years later with my youngest, Jackson, was interesting as well. I would hear "Jackson Henry" in my ear from time to time. One day, on a drive through our town, I had to go off route while following a bunch of detour signs. I ended up in front of the Jack Henry hair salon. It was so bizarre, the "detours" led me to be right in front of a place I had never seen before and there was the same name I couldn't stop hearing in my head. To this day, we usually call him Jack Henry more than we call him Jackson.

Jack was so strong and determined to come and be here. I remember going to my medium and she was like, "Oh! he's so ready to come!" before I had even conceived the little guy!

Amy: Before you were even pregnant?!

Jennifer: Yes! Eventually, after I became pregnant, I was put on bed rest because the doctors were worried he would be too premature if he didn't stop trying to get out. It was as if he didn't realize his physical body needed that time to grow and develop; he was just so ready to get into the physical world!

Ha!

He ended up bursting onto the scene a month early, but was still over 8 pounds. Thank goodness Emma, my only girl, was not so bold with her arrival almost 22 months earlier or I may have never attempted pregnancy again!

Amy: I love birth stories. They're often so telling. Do you think if you and your oldest son were able to have a dialogue about your souls and the roles they were supposed to play in this lifetime when he were younger, it would have helped you navigate your relationship better?

Jennifer: I think that's a great question. I have often thought about how helpful it would be if we could have conversations about why we interact the way we do. I wish everyone, especially kids, learned about their past lives and soul contracts because we could work through all that shit sooner, and actually have a better understanding of what our purpose is.

Like I've told you, Amy, your oldest son, Alonzo, is your most powerful teacher. He is *your* teacher and we have opportunities to fast track our growth if we can accept our teachers *wherever* they show up. Unfortunately, we get stuck in many of our most challenging relationships because of our lack of understanding. We get into power struggles because we want the hierarchy to remain intact instead of being vulnerable and open.

Amy: I can see that. My sister-in-law was the first one to call Alonzo an "old soul" when she saw him as a newborn. He's always been very mature in his mindset. Don't get me wrong, he's still a goofy kid, but he has a way of thinking that is very adult.

Jennifer: He's teaching your husband a lot too, he is like the child version of your husband, Brian. Their relationship, that dynamic, mirrors the one Brian grew up in. It is an opportunity for Brian to revisit his patterns and heal or make adjustments that call for his highest soul growth.

Amy: Yikes! I see that. It's amazing how different it feels to "parent" Alonzo versus our other two boys. He triggers us both, but I can see how on a soul level he never really accepts that he's not in charge. We call him the third parent sometimes. It's a joke, but pretty telling, too.

Jennifer: Oh my...I love it. The third parent! Too funny!

Amy: Except when three "parents" are all addressing the same issue. Then, not so funny. Uggh.

Jennifer: It may work out to recognize how he shows up in a situation. Work with it, instead of fighting it. Try to raise everyone's awareness so you're reacting consciously to one another.

Many people believe that we don't come fully formed with complete understanding of the spirit world because then we wouldn't be able to "learn our lessons" during this lifetime. I don't necessarily agree with all that. I believe that people can evolve faster when they have a deeper understanding of their past situation and how that impacts their current situation.

It's so important to avoid getting stuck in the human experience and instead stay connected to the soul/spiritual experience. If we can identify some of our soul contracts, it makes everything easier. Becoming aware or conscious is the first step to living fully.

Amy: You keep referring to "contracts."

Jennifer: Oh, whoops. Let's talk about them now.

You and I have a soul contract together that's why we latched on to one another with such ease and recognitions. Part of our work is that Jennifer's going to be the bringer of a message that Amy can act on. That's nice and all, but it didn't have to work out. Contracts are not set in stone; we have free will. You can choose to receive an opportunity or pass on it.

Think back on that first night we interacted online in that Facebook thread. You could have totally passed on my message when I delivered the message to you about writing. You could've thought I was a loon and been like, "okay, lady...you sound crazy." But you didn't!

Your growth was your knowing that the message was true. I was just the giver of the message. You had to decide what to do with this opportunity when you were at the fork in the road. You could have ignored me, but instead you decided to pursue writing...like, right away.

Amy: It's true. I'll never forget how you told me I was supposed to be a writer: you gave me some steps to get started, but you didn't exactly give me a whole new life plan. Either way, I knew what you were saying was true. I'd been an English teacher for 15 years at that point. I was always helping teens learn to write and analyze literature, but now it was *my* turn.

I can clearly see myself in my mind's eye that first night we interacted. I was sitting at the kitchen table while the boys were off playing quietly (miracle in itself) and Brian was making dinner. I called him over because I felt like your message was significant and I needed to include him. When I started to read your post aloud, I burst out in tears. It was weird, but my sweet hubby just stood there listening to me read it through all the crying.

Just for a little context: a few weeks earlier you had posted on Facebook that you were giving "free readings because your kids were too cool to hang out with you" during a snow day. I thought that post was really funny and seemed like something I would say. Without overthinking it, I commented on the thread I'd be up for a reading. First one in my life, by the way.

Jennifer: Really?!

Amy: Yes, ma'am, you were my first! I kind of knew you from social media at that point, but we could have "dated" longer, I suppose. It worked out, thankfully. In the weeks between asking for a reading and actually getting mine, I checked back on that thread. I was curious about other people's readings; I wanted to see if they were all the same or super generic.

Jennifer: Oh, gosh no. They were all so, so different... keep going I am on the edge of my seat here lol!

Amy: Well, I finished reading about how I was supposed to write; you said that it was supposed to be my #1 priority. In that moment, it felt like this powerful knowing just filled me up. It was like my soul was saying "YES" to writing.

I also heard a voice; it spoke up over my nervous brain that was worried about a big school event I was in charge of the next day. That voice said very clearly, "Tomorrow doesn't matter." Then I had a complete feeling of peace that everything was going to work out perfectly. And not even a year later, it has!

Jennifer: Yes, I love that! You were on the fast-track. That being said, if you had ignored me it might have come up again later. We have different points where we have pre-incarnation chosen to have an opportunity present itself. If something presents itself and you think, "I'm not ready to do that right now and derail my whole life plan." Don't necessarily hit the panic button and think you will never get the chance again. Sit with it for a bit and ask yourself if this is the right time and if another opportunity is set to come in the future very similar to this one. Wait for the response that feels right and true.

Amy: Or it can be as instantaneous as a punch that knocks some sense into you. I've heard of that happening to many people who make dramatic life changes. Sometimes it accompanies an illness or other tragedy.

Jennifer: So true, but many get that soul-shaking news and they still talk themselves out of it. Their egoic voice shows up and says, "That's ridiculous. Don't do that."

Amy: But if they don't talk themselves out of it, some crazy cool stuff could happen. My mom has always said that things happen for me with flow and ease. I'm starting to realize that's true because I generally listen to my gut. Or maybe it's my soul I'm listening to.

When I have a strong intuition about something I don't push it away; I follow it. My mom is the one who taught me that. She gave me permission from a very young age to trust myself even if it didn't make sense at first. Being logical and practical are not always the best ways to make decisions.

Jennifer: Ahhh! That's great. I'm so excited about this conversation because even if this book only changes the life of one person, that person will then create a ripple effect. Their shifts will then impact others and so on.

Amy: I agree, but I hope more than one person will read this book. (laughs)

Jennifer: We'll see! You just made me think about my beautiful friend Melanie who comes from a Catholic family. She was so hesitant to share her positive experience with a medium after our friend mutual friend, AJ, passed away. At first she didn't want to tell anyone about it. I reminded her that by sharing her experience she could dramatically impact someone else's life in the same positive way hers had been impacted. She eventually shared her story with some other ladies and one made an appointment with the same medium and had a lot of amazing healing happen during *her* session. It was a beautiful ripple effect. It would have been sad if Melanie kept that experience to herself.

When I think about this book and about how people could start seeing things in a different way, it gives me chills. I can see some of these topics really resonating with them. When they hear spiritual truths about themselves, they will have a familiar knowing, like, "I know that, I know that, I know that!" In that moment a change occurs and, to their core, they will never be the same again.

Amy: That's the truth. It has changed everything for me. You know, I worry that some of this could be lumped together with concepts like karma or soul contracts. Those are two things that might be helpful to discuss at this point. What do you think?

Jennifer: Hmmm. I don't love the word karma, but to that end, it's true that people have stuff they need to work out. When it comes to karma, it's best to work out in *this* lifetime.

A soul contract is a predestined (before you came into your current body) agreement that you have made with the people who are most important in your life. Each contract connects you with a specific person. Karma is different. Let's stay with contracts for bit longer.

When people choose to work with a healer or intuitive to view a soul contract that they made with a particular person, they can see if there's a way they can change it. The answer is not always yes. There's always room for revision, though. The good news is, even if it's really set in stone, you can gain an understanding as to whether it (the contract) can be carried out with love and understanding.

People find that difficult relationships that are the result of soul contracts can flow a little better with the intention for love and understanding. The easiest contracts to break are the ones that have already served their purpose. When you get to that point when you can really sense it's time to move on, you have a unique opportunity to break that particular contract and be free. In other words, it has overstayed its welcome anyways; you are just finally asking it to leave.

There are many soul contracts (and energetic cords, which we'll discuss later) that you cannot always break. There are energetic ties that you cannot sever. Here's where karma sometimes gets dragged in the mix. I've heard people say, "You went through abuse because you were the abuser in a past life." That is so irresponsible and upsetting! That kind of negativity is not what spirituality is all about.

Instead, I like the idea that you have lessons you learn during this lifetime, whether that's through ease or through challenges like abuse. What happens after a situation (positive or negative) is completely up to you. You get to decide how it transforms and catapults you to help yourself, your family, and so many other people.

Amy: This makes me a little uncomfortable because I feel bad talking about *why* people have negative experiences like abuse.

Jennifer: I agree, but I believe we have an opportunity during our human existence to use our experiences to improve the world. I would even go so far as to say we have an obligation to make a change (though not necessarily right away/today) after fulfilling any particular soul contract.

Ultimately, we have a responsibility to take even the bad experiences from our soul contracts and then help others with our gained wisdom.

Amy: Wisdom is good. I like the idea of learning, growing, and helping others.

Jennifer: Absolutely, wisdom is part of the highest good in our contracts; we are each called to do something with our experiences that will improve the world and help others. That will then raise the collective vibration of everyone in the world.

I know that we are all called to rise up and do something (it takes work to "earn" that growth) that will create shifts for humanity. The level of human evolvement that will come from those actions will be great and powerful.

Here's a personal example from my life: losing my dad when I was so young has helped me help others. It has also helped me as a parent, and helped me relate to others with their pain. I also look back at the different choices I made because of that experience good and bad: including having my son who saved me from destructive behavior. He became my lifeline. When I was pregnant with him, the sexual abuse from my childhood, which I had suppressed, came up for me. So then I addressed that abuse and healed that part of me. I realized I had a sense of urgency to heal myself for Brendan. I didn't understand it at that time, but I knew I had to find some understanding in order to be his mom.

So tying back to soul contracts again, you can have all different types of contracts, but *you* get to decide how to process them. Here's a classy example [laughing]: Let's say you've been dealt a shitty hand; *you* decide if you're going to sit in the shit or use it for manure to grow something beautiful.

Amy: Well that's an awesome and disgusting analogy... and a great place to end this discussion. Now we know the basics of soul contracts! Hopefully everyone strives to use his or her shitty situation, whether that is with people or circumstances, for manure to grow something beautiful. That will be my bedtime prayer.

Jennifer: Ha! Amen!

Amy: Alrighty. What homework do you think we should offer around soul contracts or past lives?

Jennifer: I have a great one in mind!

Homework:

Identify what topics appeal to you, but don't necessarily "make sense" with your background. These preferences don't need to be justified at this point. Focus on things that don't necessarily correlate with experiences that you've had in this lifetime. List your musical preferences, cultures that intrigue you, regions of the world, style, etc. Also list fun facts that you know or topics that you are fascinated with.

AND/ OR

Another great energy movement and awareness technique is to examine the relationships in your life. List the strongest ones: parent, child, partner, etc. Really sit with those and the dynamic each holds. Next to each name, write the strongest emotions and experiences that come up. This will create an awareness you have not consciously "known" in this life.

CHAPTER 3

Cord Cutting

Amy: What is cord cutting? It sounds weird; is it painful?

Jennifer: (laughing) Yes, it's terribly painful...ha, just kidding. Let me explain what cords are before we worry about cutting them.

We all have a life cord that connects us to human existence. This main cord is our life force; it is called the silver cord. Once that is severed the human life ends. We also have energetic cords to other people. You have cords to important people in your life like to your parents, your kids, or your spouse. Those cords can be thick and solid or thin and frayed. So when I work with people, I always ask them to "look" at their cords that are connected to others. That is not literally of course! That comes with an image in your mind's eye or just a "knowing" when you focus on what it may look like.

Amy: I like the idea of visualizing those relationships and connections in a concrete way.

Jennifer: It can be pretty powerful. When you go inward you can see those connections and understand the power and influence they have on your life.

Cords are not only formed in long-term relationships like with family and friends, you can also make energetic connections and cords in brief interactions. Even if you're in Walmart, you create very thin cord connections with people you interact with in passing. Think of Spider Man spreading thin webs: Peew...Peew...Peew. You can get hit by a cord from a total stranger.

We've all had brief, negative encounters with someone in passing that impacts our mood and then follows us long after the encounter was over. That initial interaction created a thin cord connection between you and that person. It can really bring you down if you're not careful. That being said, it can also be a positive interaction and you can feel those good feelings long after the exchange.

Amy: Like when you perform a random act of kindness? It connects you to a stranger in a positive way?

Jennifer: Yep!

Amy: I like getting those kindness cords, but I have definitely been hit by negativity out of nowhere. This conversation makes me nervous to go to the store! How can we prevent negative cords from attaching to us in the first place?

Jennifer: Excellent question! I used to feel really sick when I went to big stores like Walmart or Target. I went there on a regular basis, but it took me a long time to figure out why those trips would make me feel cruddy. This might also be happening to you when you get together with extended family or when you're in your work environment or any place that you have the potential to make consistent cord connections. The energy exchange at places or with groups you regularly visit can build up a stronger cord between you and another soul over time.

Amy: Yeah, I'm going to just stay home forever now.

Jennifer: No need, drama queen! The quickest way to protect yourself in all of these situations is to imagine an egg of protective energy around you. Really, just visualize a giant egg-shaped energy force field around you.

Then ask for assistance from God, your ancestors, angels, Jesus, your spirit guides, whomever you feel comfortable calling to your aid. Ask them to protect you from negative energies so that those cords can't influence you or attach to you. Confirm that you only want energies that are for your highest benefit to come into your energy field.

Amy: Call in the Holy Spirit, or whatever higher power you feel aligned with, and ask for a protective force field?

Jennifer: Yes!

Amy: Okay. I'm wrapping my brain around this concept. First off, I'll say it again, I like visualizing. It makes sense to me; taking something intangible and making it kind of real. Imagining an egg of protection is cool. Very Jedi-like. As a teacher, I use to tell a roomful of my squirmy students that we were each going to get inside a bubble of silence in order to focus on writing. I asked them to visualize that bubble as a safe space to work and avoid distraction. They were supposed to stay in the bubble for the duration of our free-writing time.

Jennifer: That's so cool and right in line of what I am saying. Did it work?

Amy: For the most part, yes. It helped me as a writer in public spaces when I was a student, so I was happy to see it helped them, too.

Jennifer: It's not that different from protecting yourself from unwanted cord connections. Your bubble and my egg are pretty much the same concept. I also do this for myself at night because I want a little extra love and protection while I sleep.

Amy: That reminds me of my childhood prayers at night before I'd go to bed or before I'd drive somewhere. Just setting the intention to be safe and protecting your soul from danger can be so powerful.

Jennifer: Right! But you have to ask for that assistance or protection; that's the most important part. It's less important who you ask, so long as you ask in the first place. When you're trying to decide whom to ask, stick with whatever rings true to you. For example, if you're not comfortable asking religious figures, you can ask for departed loved ones to look after you and protect you. I believe that we have free will so we must give permission for others to help us. My kids ask for a little extra guidance and comfort before they take tests at school; they let their guides know that they need it and want it.

Amy: That is so powerful! Kids need to know they have ways to get calm and centered during stressful situations. I used meditation in my classes to help my students breath, focus, and feel good before they would "show what they know" on a test. You could feel the energy in the room shift; it got much more peaceful: less squirming, tapping, etc. You can really tell when kids feel anxious... and when they feel calm.

Jennifer: I love this book because it can be used by everyone: students, teachers, parents, everyone. Divas can take what feels good to them from this conversation and pass it on to those in their lives. Super love it!!

Amy: It's funny you say that, because I was just wondering about people who will say "I don't believe any of this" and will frame their experience through a different lens. I could see my religious friends and my atheist friends both thinking this is silly.

Jennifer: To those people I'd say, you have nothing to lose! Just try it and see how you feel. Have fun and prove it wrong. Just think of all this as a little experiment!

Amy: So put an egg of protective energy around you and go out into the world and see how it goes?

Jennifer: Sure! Or don't and observe that, too. You can do everything on your own and never ask for help. See how that works out for you!

Amy: Got it. Your advice is to have fun, experiment, observe. In general, people should draw their own conclusions and see what works for them.

Jennifer: Yep! These are just tools people can use if they want and if it feels good. And truly it will resonate at a soul level, you just know.

Amy: Gotcha. So let's say I'm very onboard with the cord connections I'm making all the time. I get that I can protect myself from negativity in daily life, but let's say I have some stronger connections that are bringing me down and making it hard to have a particular person in my life. Can I just cut those cords?

Jennifer: Hmmm, it depends. You have your soul family who will show up in your life and those cords are thick and cannot be cut. They are like the iron clad soul contract peeps! On the other hand, you may have a cord or connection to an ex-lover that can still feed you negative or positive energy. When we do cord cutting we look to asking angels, especially Archangel Michael to transmute the negative into positive so you can forgive and release with love. It's important to learn the lesson of that connection while acknowledging you can sever that connection and stop all interactions that may be happening energetically.

Amy: *Learn the lesson, accept continued connection...*

Jennifer: Some people are energetically powerful and can continually re-attach to you even after you try to disconnect from them. I worked with a client who had so many people negatively connected to him that they appeared as groups of people connected to each cord instead of one individual. He was a really strong, angry man who had to sever all of these cords and he ended those energy connections; with his business partners, his ex-wife, and other negative people who had showed up. Afterwards he was so happy; like a totally different person. He told me he didn't understand what happened, but he felt so much better. What makes that story all the more interesting is he was definitely one of the people you just mentioned that thought this was crazy town. His wife had gotten him the appointment as she felt he had to try something "unconventional" due to the fact that many "traditional" things such as therapy were not working. In other words, he wasn't my most willing participant!

Amy: *I* feel better, and lighter, just hearing about that man.

Jennifer: You have to remember that negative attachments serve a purpose; they feed us in some way. Some people use it as an excuse not to move forward in their life. When you cut a cord you also remove those excuses and need to take steps into a bigger life.

Some will choose not to step into growth and will use the "this is crazy" rationale to not do it. It's much like procrastination which gives us an out if we aren't successful at something. You put off doing the work, and it may seem easier at first, but it is the exact opposite. You suffer more when you hide behind excuses and limit your chance at greatness.

Amy: Oh, I really, really get that. Like if you can be free from the excuses you usually use, you *have* to step into your greatness? I see how that can feel scary.

Jennifer: Yes, and that's why some people prefer to maintain the status quo. It's comfortable and familiar... even if it makes them feel bad, that feeling is one they feel at least I know how to live with it because I understand it.

Amy: That bums me out a bit, but I've definitely been there.

Let's shift back to folks who are ready to take action like the man you just described. I want to feel happy again.

Jennifer: Alright, missy. As I walk people through the cutting process, I always have them visualize, feel, or have an awareness of the cord. After they describe it, I ask them how they think they could "cut" it. Some people say they could use scissors; others say they'd need a chainsaw or hacksaw. That is also very telling to me about how powerful this cord has been in their lives. It's so empowering to envision yourself cutting these ties and releasing them.

Another huge part of the process is feeling where the cord is connected to you on your body. Some people will say the cord is connected to their head or their back or their stomach. Often that area will be connected with some chronic pain. Cutting the cord directly impacts that pain and shifts things for people. Side-note: I often work on the chakras, or energy centers throughout the body, associated with that area at the same time they're cutting the cord. I can do that work for people because it would be too much for them to do themselves. I can tell if a chakra is muddled or not moving. Addressing chakras with energy healing makes a big difference during this whole process. We can get into chakras more later, but they are another important part of energy healing.

Amy: I don't know why I'm thinking about this now, but how is cord-cutting like setting intentions, creating a vision board, or goal setting?

Jennifer: That's not an off-base question; it's all about getting your life to where you want it to be. I find that people tend to talk about their life, their goals or their vision board and they will say that "it's not working… it's not working" but it's usually because you have some negative energy somewhere: your past lives, with your soul contracts, with some of the negative cords, or with some really strong negative attachments. You can disconnect from those belief systems and set some loving intentions. Instead of simply learning, accepting, and believing that it's always been one way (like "all men in my family die in their forties") you can work through that, learn the lesson, and have healing. You can do the work that will allow progress in your own life. First you have to acknowledge the negativity that you feel in your life. This whole ideology that you must ignore it and immediately replace it with a positive feeling is just not true for everyone. It is important to validate your feelings and experiences and then set a new intention or reality.

Amy: That is empowering. Setting intentions by visualizing what you want and don't want; what you want to release and what you want to hold onto. I have the power!

Jennifer: You have *all* the power. You have a choice to clean the energy from your past if you want; you can even clear your present situation. Even if you cannot change the situation or sever the cord, like with a soul contract, you can still send it loving energy. You also have the ability to disassociate yourself from the thoughts and beliefs of the person you are connected to.

Amy: To recap: you can heal yourself, but it will take purposeful work to clear away the negativity and/or false beliefs that have built up over time.

Jennifer: You got it! Cord-cutting 101, baby!

Amy: I'm wondering about homework for this topic. What can readers do on their own versus what do they need support to work through?

Jennifer: You need to start thinking about where the negative cords are in your life. Divas, it's time to brainstorm.

Homework:
Make a list of everyone in your life who you feel has had a negative influence on your well-being. This can include a co-worker, a childhood bully, a former boss, a neighbor, a past lover. You do not need to limit this list to people who are currently in your life. Conduct a cord cutting for each person. See Additional Resources for instructions..

CHAPTER 4

Chakras & Crystals

Amy: We've talked about chakras in passing, but let's talk about that some more. What should people know about their chakras in general?

Jennifer: Being totally honest here, chakras can feel really overwhelming, even to try to explain sometimes. We want to make this simple, and approachable, so we are going to go back to the origin of the word and the basics.

The word **Chakra** comes from Sanskrit, meaning wheel or disc. There are seven major chakras and many minor chakras in our body. Apart from the physical body (Human), each human being has a spiritual body (Soul). This spiritual body is composed of vibrations of light (energy) and it envelops the physical body. These chakras are found embedded in our energy field. They resonate at different frequencies. The 7 major chakras, each correspond to a color in the rainbow. Chakras are spinning vortices of energy.

Amy: Vortices?

Jennifer: That's plural for vortex. A vortex is the center or hub of an energy field.

Amy: So each chakra is a separate hub of energy?

Jennifer: You got it! The location of chakras in the energy body corresponds directly to the placement of the endocrine glands in the physical body. Chakras absorb energy from your internal and external environment. In order to clear the chakras, you must access them through energy and mind. With that said, chakras have a direct effect on the state of our physical and emotional health and can impact every aspect of our life, our direction, and our decisions.

I know that sounds like a lot, but it shows you how important they really are.

Amy: That's pretty intense. I feel weird that I've never known what a chakra really was. I've heard the word before, but now that you've explained them, they sound pretty important.

Jennifer: They are definitely important! You are not the only one who has been surprised that you didn't know what they were, myself included. We have to remember we don't know something until we come across information or a person who introduces us, but once we know it is up to us to explore it further and get balanced. When you get everything spinning and going smoothly with your chakras, you can really "step into the vortex" of your life; things just feel more balanced. Think of them as the gateway to your soul!

Amy: Yes, please. I want that. Hello, gateway to my soul! Here I come.

Jennifer: Everyone wants that ease and flow. We all want to be in the vortex! Let's talk about how each chakra works:

Crown (*white*, at the top of your head)- a source of healing, protection, enlightenment, and spiritual connection. Knowledge and Understanding.

Issues with connection to your spirituality and your beauty is rooted here.

This chakra deals with pure cosmic energy and is blocked by earthly attachment.

The closest "physical" connection is to the pituitary gland.

I love the Crystal Quartz, Calcite, Selenite, and Herkimer stones for this chakra.

Third-Eye (*purple*, right between your two eyes)- the center for intuition. Imagination comes from this place as well. I think of this as the "command center".

Issues with making decisions are rooted here.

This chakra deals with insight and is blocked by illusion.

The closest "physical" connection is to the pineal gland.

I love an Amethyst, Sodalite, Angelite, and Kyanite stones for this chakra.

Throat (*blue*, your throat area)- the center of verbal expression where we speak our highest truth. Communication and creativity.

Speaking your truth issues are rooted here.

This chakra deals with truth and is blocked by lies.

The closest "physical" connection is to your thyroid.

I love Blue Lace Agate, Lapis Lazuli, Turquoise, and Aquamarine stones for this chakra.

Heart (*green*, your chest)- the bridge between the lower and upper chakras; our body and soul; source of love and connection. Love and relationships.

Inner peace and ability to love issues are rooted here.

This chakra deals with love and is blocked by grief.

The closest "physical" connection is to your Thymus.

I love Green Aventurine, Rose Quartz, Malachite, Jade and Fluorite stones for this chakra.

Solar Plexus (*yellow*, bottom of ribcage to belly button)- the center of our personal power.

Self-worth and self-confidence issues are rooted here.

This chakra deals with willpower and is blocked by shame.

Closest "physical" connection is to adrenal glands.

I love Citrine, Topaz, Amber, and Moonstone stones for this chakra.

Sacral (*orange*, reproductive area)- our sexual center and source of creativity and creative expression. Emotions and Sensuality.

Sexual issues and overall well-being are rooted here

This chakra deals with pleasure and is blocked by guilt

Closest "physical" connection is to the sacral vertebrae.

I love Carnelian, Jasper, Garnet, and Ruby stones for this chakra.

Root (*red*, base of your spine)- basis of stability, security, and our basic needs, this comes up a lot when we explore people's past. This includes childhood *and* past lives. It is foundation of our patterns and belief system. Financial problems are rooted here.

This chakra deals with survival and is blocked by fear.

Closest "physical" connection is to the reproductive organs.

I really love Smoky Quartz, Black Obsidian, Hematite, and Tiger's Eye stone for this chakra.

Amy: That's a great guide to chakras. I am going to come back to this section again and again to remind myself which chakra I need to focus on.

Jennifer: It's so important to understand these concepts in general, instead of fixating on the details like the exact color or area. As always, it's so key to focus on the intention of your healing.

Amy: That's fascinating in and of itself; it makes me want to go and meditate and focus on the particular area and energy field that I want to heal.

Jennifer: I love this conversation because it is about *your* healing! It also brings us to an awareness of *other* people's healing and moves us beyond the one person's body and energy. It's more about healing the interlocking and alignment of the energy of more people. Which in turn connects us all on a higher level to one another!

Amy: Oh, I like that!

Jennifer: I got this next message of connection that I want to share while I was in a float tank and during an Amethyst meditation on my 40th birthday this year. I was in and out of my body through the whole experience. It was wild! There was so much information it was like overload central! The main message I got is how we're supposed to be getting in balance *with* other people. It's not about just healing ourselves.

Amy: The connection idea is so comforting; you're not alone in "fixing" stuff. I like the idea of getting alignment with my husband Brian. We've been together for 18 years, but I understand how we are still a work in progress.

Jennifer: Yes, but we all are! I kept hearing from Source that "it is not that hard". Meaning we make it far too difficult to understand these concepts and this connection to everything. We almost make it unattainable or that we have to be an "expert" in order to utilize this in our human experience. The spirit world wants us to understand that all of this spiritual connection is easy; it's not meant to be difficult. It is who we are. We are spiritual beings having a human experience.

Amy: So we can take steps to balance our chakras on our own? That seems like a good first step so that we can balance with others.

Jennifer: You definitely can. Remember, *you* have the power and it isn't meant to be difficult. If you want to start with an action step, begin working with your chakras. Start with stones or crystals with the colors that coordinate with the colors of each chakra: red, orange, yellow, green, blue, purple, and white. (remember colors of the rainbow- easy!) and simply hold them.

You can even buy chakra bags with the seven co-ordinating stones. You can even order them online, just type in key-words "chakra stones" or visit your local crystal shop or metaphysical store.

When my youngest son was eight years-old he had a bag of chakra stones and he put them on each of the chakras on his body and laid on his bed or the ground to let himself recharge. This isn't just for grown-ups; kids benefit from getting back in balance. Kids don't need a big explanation either, just experiment with having them pick out some stones or put ones you have on them and just have them lay down with them on for a short time. We all want to feel good and this is an easy activity!

Amy: I want to do that and show my boys how to do it, too. Most of the time when I need to recharge, I usually reach for coffee. For some reason that doesn't always energize me, so I'm totally open to alternatives and this seems like an easy, "hell, yeah" option.

Jennifer: You need to reboot your energy with crystals, momma!

Amy: I love looking at crystals, they are so pretty, but I don't really understand how they're supposed to work for me. You can tell me anything basic because I don't know enough to ask a good question here.

Jennifer: Okay, let's start of acknowledging that we all have intuition; a sense of knowing. Even if you can't explain it, you'll often have a sense of what you want to do, who you want to talk to, or where you should sit in any particular situation.

If you are looking at a display of stones and crystals in a shop, you will naturally be drawn to some more than others. Assuming they were different shapes and sizes you would probably have feelings about which ones you feel most attracted to.

When I went shopping with my Aunt Jeanne, and she was looking at all of the pretty stones and asked what each one "did" and I realized we were going about it all wrong. I stopped her questions and asked her what she would want to heal in her life right now. Once we identified which crystal coordinated with her area of concern, I asked her to choose a specific stone that she felt particularly drawn to.

Amy: Just to recap: she set the intention, brought forth the situation she wanted healed, and did a little research to see which crystals could help with that. Then she opened herself up to what she was attracted to...and picked up one particular crystal out of all the many, many crystals before her?

Jennifer: Yes, exactly!

Amy: That seems less intimidating that way. I could do that.

Jennifer: Of course you could! Everyone can! We don't need to make the intuitive process difficult, it's *our* intuition! It is already a natural part of our existence. We just need to call forth our intentions, ask for help from our guides, and then actually trust ourselves to find the perfect match.

Amy: Love it!

Jennifer: There are specific crystals for specific uses beyond chakra work. For example, selenite is in every corner of my house. In fact, I have a wand in front of me right now. This particular crystal helps with protection and healing.

Amy: We bought some of those when Brian wasn't feeling well and a different intuitive healer recommended them. I remember you telling me how much you like them, too.

Jennifer: Yes, it's great for creating a sacred space in your home, even just a little space. Don't overwhelm yourself here. I find that if people think they can't do it big or "right" they won't do it at all. Don't make it a stressful undertaking! Find small ways to incorporate crystals into your life. Make it easy!

Amy: Oh, that makes me think about things I already have. Are salt lamps considered a crystal? I love my salt lamps and I have them all over the house.

Jennifer: Yes, ma'am. I actually get asked quite a bit about salt lamps and why they are beneficial etc. Let me give a little background. Salt lamps are made with Himalayan crystals. Himalayan crystal salts are primarily a storage medium for life force energy. It is the most beneficial and cleanest salt on this planet. It was formed about 250 million years ago where the energy of the sun had dried up the original, primal sea. It contains all the elements found in our bodies. Having these lamps really balances the environment around you. Bonus, they aren't expensive!

Another little tip: Buy some Pink Himalayan salt. You can buy Pink Himalayan salt right in the same aisle you purchase your regular salt. It's really great to grind the crystals for everyday salt use and you can put some in your drinking water for added health benefit.

Amy: I'm glad that I use Pink Himalayan salt for cooking already. I didn't know you should put it in water. I've heard a pinch of salt in a glass of water changes the flavor enough to make it palatable even for people who say they don't "like" drinking water.

Jennifer: You should definitely try it; it raises your energetic vibration. Easy breezy! Back to salt lamps, they are great for purifying the room and getting the negativity out of the space. Ironically they emit negative ions that balance out the positive ions that are emitted from technology like computers, cell phones, and microwaves. That is something we often don't give much thought to because technology is such a part of our lives, but all those tech ions aren't good for us.

Amy: I knew that they were pleasant to have around, but I didn't know all that about technology. What other everyday stones or crystals are good to know about?

Jennifer: Let me think of some that we have around the house. My son's hematite rings are so responsive. Hematite absorbs negativity and then usually breaks once the maximum negativity it can absorb has been reached. My oldest son Brendan's rings would always break because he's such a strong empath, but didn't protect himself. He was always absorbing negativity during his teenage years: his own stuff and the negativity of others so within days each ring would break. Arrgh!

Amy: What is an empath? How should empaths like your son protect themselves?

Jennifer: Empaths are people who take on other people's emotions. They may feel certain emotions that don't really belong to them. They are sponges for other people's "stuff" and since most empaths don't understand what's happening, they don't protect themselves from all that extra emotional baggage. They take it on as their own, which can be really bad. It is so important to learn how to properly protect yourself, think back to the egg of protection and calling in your guides we talked about earlier. This one step is super easy and even more necessary for empaths. It can be such a huge benefit to an empath or for those who help others. You have to be able to keep other people's stuff from invading your space. Think like Patrick Swayze in Dirty Dancing, "this is my space, this is your space."

Amy: Oh, that makes me want to watch the movie again. I get that analogy. You can still "dance" together energetically, but you never want someone crowding you.

Jennifer: Exactly. Think about how enjoyable dancing is when there are smooth and fluid movements versus someone stepping on your toes every other step or pressing their bodies too close to yours, hello boundaries! Well unless that is what you want!

Amy: I have more questions about crystals now. Just when I thought I didn't know enough to ask you anything, all the sudden I have a bunch of questions.

Jennifer: Oh good, ask away!

Amy: Does it matter if a crystal is in jewelry, in a certain shape, smooth or rough? What is the difference between a crystal and a stone?

Jennifer: Some crystals are more like raw clusters and when I think of stones they are more polished like they went through a tumbler. I personally feel more connected to the ones that are spiky, raw, like they just came out of the Earth. I hold an amethyst that is very raw and substantial when I work with someone. Again, don't overthink any of this, it is a stone or a crystal. Whatever you want to call it.

Amy: I really love amethyst. That was my preferred stone when I was growing up so I always got jewelry with it. I remember several amethyst rings.

Jennifer: Oh, really?! I have such a personal connection with amethyst, too. It has served me well in so many situations. I remember when I couldn't sleep and I got a message from my guides to get out my huge amethyst cathedral crystal. It's huge! I was told to put it near my head which I thought would be impossible, but when I got it out and put it on the shelf next to my bed, it ended up being exactly the same height as where my head lays on the pillow. I felt a ringing right away in my ear and the energy was a bit overwhelming due to the size of it, but I passed out and slept better than I had in weeks. Thank you guides!

Amy: That's awesome. So many people would love that type of relief: sleep without medication!

Jennifer: I know it. This was a particularly hard time for me. My friends who are also intuitive told me that my recently deceased friend, AJ, and my dad were on either side of me trying to help me get clarity in that moment. And rest.

After that, I felt like it was easier to connect with my intuitive side. Previously, right after AJ's death, I felt so cut-off. Grief had shut it all down. This was a real turning point for me.

Amy: So you think the Amethyst Cathedral rebooted you, in a sense?

Jennifer: Oh yeah. It was the beginning of a really important shift for me. That next morning, I felt like I took a true breath for the first time in weeks. Many times what we are going through in our lives makes even thinking about rebooting an overwhelming task in itself. If we just remain a little open to feel those gentle nudges the Universe sends our way, there are answers waiting for us.

For me, it was the combination of finally getting sleep and connecting with that big powerful crystal while I slept. That experience was so powerful for me. Being around crystals, especially carrying them with you, is such an easy way to find peace.

Amy: I'd love to do that, but there are days I don't have any pockets. #girlproblems

Jennifer: Women often put crystals in their bra. It's called "packing" and then we will ask each other, "Hey, girl, what are you packing today?" Too funny!

Amy: Really?

Jennifer: Girl, yes! Rose Quartz is a powerful crystal that a lot of people need because it supports your heart chakra. You can put a small one in your bra and hit the road. Green also goes with your heart chakra (Emerald); remember you can also put that in your pillowcase while you sleep. Rose Quartz will help you with any pain you have, just hold the stone as you ask for help. It's also important to take time to acknowledge the healing you want to have in that chakra and put the stone close to that area, whether that means sitting on them or holding them.

Amy: Now that you mention it, I had a crystal on my lap as I finished my first book. I was working for long stretches at a time and it was with me throughout. I don't remember which one it was. I just picked it up and decided to have it near me.

Jennifer: That's lovely! Why do you think you picked that particular stone?

Amy: I'm not sure. I think you told me once to just close my eyes and feel each stone and choose the one I felt most connected to in that moment. I think I needed a little help with my concentration as I did the final leg of my writing. It was by my side literally and energetically the whole time. It held the space for me to concentrate.

Jennifer: Perfect! Crystals are great for so many different reasons; some crystals are good for activating your own intuition. Some are especially good for reconnecting with your inner guidance. They're also really powerful when used during meditation.

Amy: Oh, I can do that! I can select a crystal or two before I meditate. Good tip!

Jennifer: Remember we want to "clean" and "charge" our crystals from time to time. You clean them by getting some sage or some people call them smudge sticks. You can order one online or in a shop and then burn some in a room where you want to clear the energy. Hold your crystals over the smoke to clear them for future use.

You can also charge them under a full moon. I just put mine outside or on a windowsill.

Amy: How do they charge? Why do they need to be cleaned?

Jennifer: Like I told my friend (from the intro), the moon is a guidance system for us and it is a source of energy. When the moon is full, it releases the most energy.

If our crystals are in its presence during this time, they will absorb and transmute that energy. It's also important to clear the heavy energy that may have been accumulated over time, that's why we clean them. Crystals need a reboot just like they can help reboot us!

Amy: Okay, let's connect it all; how are crystals connected to chakras?

Jennifer: Crystals help us balance our energies and our chakras are our energy centers. Make sense?

Amy: Got it.

Jennifer: Crystals are so inexpensive. This is a really easy way to try something new without breaking the bank. You have nothing to lose!

Amy: I want to get the bag of chakra crystals that your son used.

Jennifer: You should, do you feel confident using them?

Amy: I do now! I want to show my kids how to use them, too.

Homework:

Go over the chakra descriptions in this chapter and identify what emotions or difficulties you have in your life that fall into some of the "symptoms" of a chakra that is out of balance.

AND / OR

Make it a priority to visit online or a local metaphysical store to get your own healing stones.

AND / OR

Sit with these stones and give some focused attention to these areas in your life and ask for assistance.

AND / OR

Do chakra clearing and balancing meditation.

CHAPTER 5

Card Reading

Amy: I want to learn more about card readings. Are there different types of cards?

Jennifer: Oooh, cards are fun. Yes, there are different kinds of cards. We can talk about all of that.

Amy: I also get confused when I hear people say they "clean their cards" before using them. Can we add that to the convo, too?

Jennifer: Of course! Let's start with what we mean by "cards" There are so many different cards around these days it is hard to pin it down to one blanketed name. How about we go with guidance cards. These are the cards that used to be referred to as tarot cards. Now they have all kinds of names: angel cards, wisdom cards, animal guides, past life, the list goes on and on.

Much the same as with crystals/stones if you feel drawn to learn more about these you will be drawn to the guidance cards that are best suited for you at this time. If you continue to use guidance cards, you will find you are drawn to get new ones as things shift and your intuition grows.

Okay. Now to cleaning your cards. Cleaning your cards is a little different than cleaning crystals. I got my first set of *tarot* cards when I was in middle school, if you can believe that! Wow. that was a long time ago and I was young now that I am thinking back about it. Anyway, I did this whole thing where I slept with them under my pillow to connect with the energy.

Amy: Wow, you slept with them?

Jennifer: Yep, that's just the type of girl I am! I wanted to become one with them. Ha! I also to this day I MUST touch each and every card when I get a new deck. I just flip through the deck one at a time and touch them. It's like I'm saying, "hey, there!" to each of them. It works for me.

Amy: I understand how that would connect them to you, but how will it help if I'm getting a reading from someone who is using their own deck? Won't the energy be connected to them alone?

Jennifer: Yes, but when I do card readings for other people I ask questions on behalf of them. I asked to be used in service of the message that is meant to be shared.

Amy: That makes sense to me. I see how you're always establishing boundaries or setting intentions before doing any energy work. It's the same when you work with cards, I guess. Does everyone who reads cards have the same routine?

Jennifer: No, I feel like every single person has their own way of working with cards, just as each person is unique. In the process of obtaining my certification as an Ordained Spiritual Healer, I learned the traditional methods of the tarot. Although I had used cards for years, it was really interesting to go back to the basics the way someone who had never touched a card would experience. One thing I've learned on my own is that I must pick a deck that resonates with *me*. Whether you are drawn to angels, fairies, chakras, Native American culture, etc. you are sure to find a deck that speaks to you. Start there. Trust your instinct from the beginning when you choose a deck.

One thing I would encourage you to do is look at the card and see what comes to you before you open the accompanying book to read the description. Using both your own natural intuition, as well as the book description, really feels good to people.

Amy: How so?

Jennifer: After you pull a card, you can read what the book says or what's written on the card itself. That being said, I still recommend first establishing your energetic relationship with the card(s). When I first got my cards when I was 13, I got them in a silk wrap and, like I said earlier, I put them under my pillow and slept with them and then I touched every card to connect. Now, since I am much older and more experienced, I also sage each one; each and every one.

Amy: Does that take forever?

Jennifer: Not really, I only do it the first time I use a deck. I just pass one card through the smoke one at a time. You can do it pretty quickly. After that, I put my hand over the whole deck and pass the entire deck through the sage smoke if I'm doing it for someone else.

Amy: I'm not sure if this feels more complicated or pretty easy. I'm still undecided.

Jennifer: It's not hard, maybe I'm making it sound more difficult that it is. Let's just do something really quick. Here, I'll pull a card for you: 3 of chalices …. The picture on the card is a woman with a flower headband with a man and woman behind her. Friendships, networking and roots are super, super important for you right now.

Next card: 7 of chalices with a staircase (that I often see in my dreams) that I know for me to be the staircase to another dimension, there are also cups with a book, a crown, man and woman looking to each other, castle, coins, lots of different energy. It's so obvious that this is a card all about your life. A lot of times your card reading is a validation of your current path. I see money, relationships, home on each step. It seems clear to me that you're basically on level 6 ...so what you're looking for next in your life is spiritual enlightenment. You're going up the stairs in life.

The next thing you can do is look at the images and see what it says to you as the reader. I put my energy into that and ask for answers and validation for you. Then I stay open to whatever thoughts, feelings, or images come to me. I might glance at the book that accompanies that deck to see what jumps out at me on the page that corresponds with that particular card. I never just read what's preprinted in the book. That is just me. When you skim, whatever you need to see jumps out at you. That is an amazing intuitive tool for everyone; just stay open to what stands out as you glance over it all.

Amy: A lot of that felt great. I have a deck that I pull a card and read what it says on that particular card. It has been somewhat meaningful. The images don't resonate with me very much, though.

Jennifer: Then get a different deck, honey!

Amy: That's not frivolous? Just jumping from deck to deck?

Jennifer: Uh, no! You need to find one that lights you up. I have different decks for different occasions, too.

Amy: Can you tell me what *you* look for in a deck?

Jennifer: Actually, I was at a bookstore this week and I was looking at the cards and they have so many different decks: animal totem, angels, etc. I love that section, and I always visit it when I go to that store. I was looking for a deck, but on this particular trip, I wasn't drawn to anything. So I didn't get one. I don't get a deck because it's a good price or anything like that. If I don't get drawn to a deck, I don't get it. On the other hand, one time I saw a Doreen Virtue deck about past lives and I felt like, "I have to have them!" so I bought them and they are amazing. You have to have that connection; that pull, that feeling like "you are meant to be mine."

Amy: Now I'm feeling more confident, almost feel like I could do card readings for myself instead of asking someone else to do them for me.

Jennifer: Exactly! One client said to me, "What I started coming to you for, I found I could do for myself." I thought that was so great because once you learn to trust yourself you can build on your own intuition. But it's also good to seek outside guidance and support if you feel drawn to that. In fact, I do that. A healer needs healing, too. I have a person that I go to, the same person for twenty years, who I trust to help me when things don't feel aligned.

My goal is to let people know they can get help,

but they don't have to go outside of themselves for answers and validation.

Amy: Why do people need cards versus just connecting straight to source?

Jennifer: I don't use them often, but sometimes I'm drawn to cards. I have a strong ability to tap into messages, but many people can't...yet. Everyone has the ability to receive messages directly, it is just a matter of doing things like cards and energy work to remind you what you already know. I will keep saying it, YOU have all of the power.

When you work with cards, you decide how you want to organize them based on the information you are looking to receive. There are different ways to display cards, a couple of examples are a "one card pull" or a "full spread".

Amy: What's the difference between a one card pull and a full spread?

Jennifer: A one card pull is what we were just talking about: when you pull a single card in response to a question or just a card-of-the-day. Sometimes you grab a card because you feel drawn to do so, without any other reason. Many people love to get their deck out and just pull a message or guidance for the day. Super fun and a great way to stay connected not only to your deck, but to yourself.

A full card reading is a specific series of cards that represent your past, present, future, challenges, outcomes. Important note: I always ask my guides to place the cards in the order that are in line with the questions I am asking.

Cards that represent "Past" help you build trust with the cards, in general. If that card shows you something that resonates with you, then you know you can believe the next card that will give you the message about your "future." We call this process "the order of trust" because it helps you to connect, or trust, your cards.

Traditional decks have books with spreads (series of cards) that you can reference. I know this may seem overwhelming or even confusing. I want to give an easy introduction, but there is really no way to explain it in a way that can be fully understood in such few words. The good news is this chapter should make you want to run out and get your own deck and find your own rhythm!

Amy: I'm definitely not comfortable doing a spread yet, but I like the idea of a one card pull. I kind of already do that.

Jennifer: You may be surprised. You may start hearing words, getting feelings and messages as you scroll through the cards. Channeled messages are so important; you really have to stay present and aware.

Amy: Okay, I'll try it. While I am getting more and more comfortable with the idea of doing a reading for myself, it still feels strange to think about pulling cards for someone else. How do you filter when you should tell people the messages you receive?

Jennifer: Good question. If you ask permission first that can help someone shift to a receiving mode. If someone comes to me and asks for help and requests that I'm blunt; then I'm blunt. I always get a little uncomfortable when I know I'm saying something hard for the receiver to hear. I understand it's not a feel-good message, but I try to be an open channel. Even if people ask for and pay for something, there will be those who resent you because of the message.

Amy: That happens in "real life," too. I'll feel the need to tell someone something, but I have a sense that it will be a hard thing to for them to process. Or, sometimes I feel the need to share something and I'm not really sure what it means or where the message is coming from.

Jennifer: If you feel like you have a strong message to share with someone, cards involved or not, tell the person how you feel and ask if you can share with them. Then, silently, ask their guides to be present to help them to receive the message.

Amy: Okay, but it's still risky.

Jennifer: Of course it is; welcome to my world! When you go to get a reading you have to decide if you're open to the messages that are going to come through no matter what they are. I've learned that a lot of people are looking for the answer they *want* instead of the truth. They will search everywhere and ask, and ask, and ask, all kinds of different people until they hear the "perfect" response. The one they *want* to hear. Think about when you ask for guidance from casual friends versus close friends.

Most likely, the close friends will tell you the truth, but not necessarily what we "want to hear." Sometimes this makes us want to jump from friend to friend until we hear an answer that we wanted. If you fish around until you find the "fish" you want, you'll feel better, I guess, but you won't get the truth.

Amy: That makes sense to me. I've definitely done that. I get frustrated with friends who disagree with my "story" about a situation and I then find their advice tough to take. On the flip side, I feel icky when I get the answer I want but I know it's not really the truth. I want to change the truth, but I can't.

Jennifer: That's where the growth is! You need to acknowledge the truth so you can learn and grow from facing it. That's why people need to be honest about why they're going for a reading; to affirm everything they're already doing or to hear how they can grow and evolve.

Amy: That's why everything feels off until you just acknowledge what's real.

Jennifer: It's more about finding your own intuition.

If you have a solid understanding of your own intuition, then you will be able to "hear" the truth and make peace with it more easily. Being conscious of your inner guidance helps you recognize authentic guidance when it presents itself.

Amy: That feels really good to me. Again, I have the power!

Jennifer: If that's the one message Divas hear in this book, I'm happy.

Amy: It seems like everything we are discussing comes back to getting in touch with your own intuitive nature so that you can find alignment. A lot of these other topics are specific tools that you can use to get back in spiritual alignment...

Jennifer: ...ahhhhh, yes, alignment!!

Amy: Alright, it's homework time. What should we work on now? Can we suggest everyone find a deck of cards that are calling their name?

Jennifer: Sure!

Homework:

Go to the "new age" section of a bookstore like Barnes&Noble or go online and search "tarot" and look through what they offer and have fun exploring. Buy a deck that you feel drawn to.

Once you get a deck, take some time to take them out of the box and touch each card. You can also hold them over some burning sage and ask that the cards will provide you with inspiration and insights. Use this time to connect with your cards. Relax and enjoy this "me" time. No rushing!

When you're ready to pull a card, don't put any stress on yourself or worry about right or wrong answers. Have a calm, open energy when you select your cards. Look at each card and see what thoughts, images or feelings come up for you. Give yourself space to experience any wisdom that may come forth.

Remember: you don't have to ever pull cards for someone else; instead, just work to develop your own intuition.

CHAPTER 6

Deceased Loved Ones & Spirit Guides

Amy: I'm excited about this next topic! How can our deceased loved ones and spirit guides show up in our life?

Jennifer: Your enthusiasm is too funny! I love it!

Let's start with a real-life story: a client sent me a pic with a white feather in her hand. It was the fourth white feather she had found in a matter of days. Before working with me she said she wouldn't have even noticed a feather, but now it felt different. She wondered where it came from; who "sent" it. Even though she didn't know what the white feather meant, she said it was very comforting.

It's important to note that this particular client came into my life many years earlier when her older son played football with my son. She and I did not stay in physical contact over the years, but we are friends on

Facebook. At some point I saw her post about her struggles with fibromyalgia. I felt led to respond and commented that she should look into reiki. She messaged me that she didn't know what that even was, but was willing to try.

Amy: That's why we're having this public "conversation," people don't know what they don't know! She became your client for reiki even though she didn't even know that type of energy work existed when she put out her original post.

Jennifer: I know...and things are about to get even more interesting. During the first reiki session in her living room, I saw fire while I was in front of her fireplace. Then I saw a blonde man who died in a fire on his birthday. I immediately checked with my guides: Am I thinking of this fire because I'm here in front of the fireplace? My guidance said "no" and quickly after information was shown to me that someone gave the blonde guy something that made him sleepy which is why he died in the fire. His wife and children had made it out, but he didn't.

Once I told my client, she was startled because she said I was describing the death of one of her family members. This is one of those times a person might hesitate to deliver the message as it is not only emotional, it is also accusatory.

Later she contacted me because she found a diamond bracelet in the living room. She thought it was mine, but I assured her it wasn't. It gave her pause because she couldn't figure out where the bracelet had come from. I next asked her when the blonde family member's birthday was. She responded, "April" (birthstone: diamond) I then asked how old he was when he died. She responded. I told her to please count the number of diamonds on the bracelet.

Amy: Don't tell me the number of diamonds matched his age!

Jennifer: You guessed it, the number of diamonds represented the age he was when he passed.

I've since realized that her fibromyalgia may have been the link that brought me to her house and the message to her from her loved one, but I knew the whole thing was divinely planned by her loved one. Which leads back to the four feathers she found. It was only after we worked together and she found the bracelet, that she was open to the message of the feathers being a message of comfort from her departed loved ones.

Amy: Was there anything more to the feathers?

Jennifer: No, the white feathers felt significant to her and she paid attention when she wouldn't have previously, that is what the takeaway is. The fact that you're seeing something that feels powerful and actually acknowledging it is key. So many people miss signs because they aren't open to them or they dismiss them. Cardinals are often considered signs from loved ones. My friend, Melanie, felt like our deceased friend AJ was not connecting with her. She later realized she was looking at a cardinal as she was saying that. She called me and told me how comforting that was to her.

I've had complex signs present themselves in my life in unique ways. For example, my friend, Olivia, called me because she had a dream where AJ told her to give me a book of matches. Unbeknownst to her, I had been repeatedly listening to an old song from the 90's, called "Matches." That simple, but strange, exchange reminded me of AJ.

But that isn't the craziest part, get ready for this… Olivia lives in another state and flew in the day after AJ passed. When I picked her up from the airport she wanted to go to a place called The Broken Spoke that I had never been to. The first line of the song, "Matches," that I had been listening to was, "We met at The Broken Spoke."

In the end, the matchbook he had told her to give me in that dream was such an important symbol for me. The first night I met AJ, I wrote my name and number in a book of matches and gave it to him. It was the late '90s when I first met him, so this was how you gave someone your info back then.

For me, this series of events was a beautiful message that connected all three of us. He guided me to listen to that old song over and over and then delivered this dream message to show he was right there with us at The Broken Spoke after he passed, all that in addition to the matches that first connected us.

Amy: I really understand how all of those things made sense to you and resonated with your memories of AJ. It hurts my heart to think about how we sometimes ignore those messages when they are given to us for comfort as we are healing.

Jennifer: You can receive a message from a deceased loved one any way, any where, any time, and through anyone.

Here is another recent example for you; my mom recommended a book that Anderson Cooper co-wrote with his mother about his brother's suicide, she thought it could help me deal with AJ's death, but I dismissed it. Not long after that, my kids and I were driving to school listening to the radio. Every Monday morning a woman does a movie review. She disliked the movie she was reviewing so much that she decided to recommend a book she read over the weekend instead, something I had never heard her do. The book? "The Rainbow Comes and Goes," which is the book by Anderson Cooper that my mom had just mentioned. So in that moment I knew that I had to read it. I knew that this book would have an important role in my healing since it presented itself twice so distinctly. Like I said, messages can come in any way, any where, any time, and through any one.

Amy: It's nice to think about unseen powers conspiring in our favor; looking out for us.

Jennifer: That has actually always been the reality, but we have to allow that help to be present in our lives. Too often we are closed off and determined to do things "our way" which is very limiting.

Amy: I never thought about that. So many of us pride ourselves on doing everything on our own. How exhausting!

Jennifer: Totally! With help from your angels or guides or whatever you feel the need to call forth, there is so much more ease in life. Remember, we have to *ask* for help if we truly want their assistance. We have to make a concerted effort to request support with confidence, whether it's for an important decision we need to make, protection, guidance, healing, etc. You have an army of spiritual helpers who are eager to assist when you need them. You have free will to live the life you want, but if you want help, your guidance is always there for assistance. When I ask for help, the right people and situations fall into place. I can instantly feel a shift.

Amy: I love that. I think the asking for help and protection makes sense.

Jennifer: I ask for protection all the time. In fact, I've been told that it's hard to tap into my energy because I have an "army" of protection surrounding me. And I say, "I know, I do that on purpose. I don't allow just anyone into my energy"

When I ask for protection and guidance I always start with "Father, Mother, God, First Creator" to cover the higher powers in my existence. I don't know where that intro came from, but I feel called to invite male and female.

Amy: Praying for an army of protection is an awesome concept. It's something we all do starting as young kids: with bedtime prayers, before we eat, in preparation for big test. I need to start praying like that again.

Jennifer: Yes, before I go to sleep I ask that whatever energies I encounter as I sleep be of the highest vibration, the best intentions, the truest form on a soul level, and in a familiar physical form.

So many people say our dreams are from the sub-conscious, but I believe that when we sleep we can travel through time and space at a soul level. We must protect ourselves fully before embarking on the sleep state journey.

Amy: What should we work on now? Should we start to notice things with a new perspective? Maybe look for the signs that present themselves to us and stay open to the messages they bring.

Jennifer: The best piece of advice I can give here is to not look too hard or have expectations that are too high. Don't put too much pressure on yourself. Instead, just stay open and allow.

Homework:

Before going to bed think about something you have been needing guidance on. This can be something you haven't told anyone about or something you have told everyone about. Ask to be given guidance during your sleep state. Do this every night for a week.

AND / OR

See what comes up differently than what others have told you or what you have told yourself. Look for new ideas and people that come into your life during and after the week.

AND / OR

Set the intention that you are open to receive signs. Remain open and allow.

AND / OR

During waking hours ASK in your mind or out loud (whichever feels more natural for you) for your guides and spiritual family to assist you. Give them permission to do so.

CHAPTER 7

Synchronicity

Amy: How does synchronicity work in our lives?

Jennifer: Let's start with numbers. Numbers are the most obvious ways synchronicities show up in our lives. For example; My oldest son Brendan's number has always been 333. He says that when he is off or imbalanced in his life, he won't see that number. But when he starts seeing it on license plates or the clock, etc. he knows he's in alignment. It's like a reminder that you are following your guidance and that you're in flow or in the vortex.

Amy: I see 11:22 a lot. That's my hubby's birthday so I always text him: "11:22, I love you!" I'm always tickled when I see it. Even if we are not really vibing as a couple, I still somehow happen to look at the clock right at that particular time. I don't necessarily feel mushy towards him at those times, but it reminds me how connected we are. Numbers can really emphasize that spiritual connection.

Jennifer: Yes! Did you know that 11, 22 is a sacred number, too?

Amy: No. Really? How do you know what's sacred and what's just a number?

Jennifer: I am always looking up numbers that I see repeatedly. It's pretty easy these days to just do a quick search on Google. These special numbers are called angel numbers online, so I search "Angel number *whatever the number is*"

There are a few different sites that give amazing descriptions of angel numbers. If you notice things that seem significant like when I see a license plate that says something like IM 452 VIJEN it speaks to me. It isn't necessarily numbers that are the same such as the 333. If I see a number again and again, like 452, on the odometer or a digital clock that speaks to me, I look it up. It can give you such a boost and get you to a high vibe. It's never negative, but they're encouraging whispers about how your life is going. Whenever you take the time to notice the synchronicities with numbers, you put yourself in a space of receiving. My friend's death certificate had nothing but 9s on it. 9 here, 9s there. This is the year of 9

(2016=2+0+1+6=9) and that's also the number of endings.

Start noticing numbers on your receipts, gas pumps, clocks, license plates, etc. The timer on the commercial I watched the other day said 555 which the number 5 speaks about change. It can change your life because once you start seeing synchronicity it can heighten your awareness and give you the connection to the Universe.

Since you and your hubby both have birthdays on the 22nd of the month, why don't you go look up 22.

Amy: Okay...got it. It's kind of long but all really uplifting.

> *Number 22 brings the attributes of number 2 appearing twice, amplifying its influences. Number 2 relates to your **Divine life purpose and soul mission**, duality and balance, partnership and relationships, diplomacy and adaptability, insight, sensitivity and selflessness. Master Number 22 carries the energies and attributes of diplomacy, intuition and emotion, balance and harmony, adaptability, diplomacy, personal power, redemption, idealism, expansion and evolution, idealism, philanthropy and service and duty and **manifesting your highest ideals and desires**. Number 22 is a number of power and accomplishment.*
>
> *Angel Number 22 encourages you to work diligently on your spiritual life path and **soul purpose**.*

*Angel Number 22 brings a message from your **angels** that you are to take a balanced, harmonious and peaceful stance in all areas of your life. Stand strong in your personal convictions and act accordingly. You have a great deal to achieve, and with devotion and **inner-wisdom** you will be able to **successfully manifest your desired results.***

Angel Number 22 can turn the most ambitious of dreams into reality. Angel Number 22 asks you to see the larger picture, and to work with the details necessary to complete that picture. Angel Number 22 encourages you to bring things through to fruition on both the spiritual and material planes.

*Angel Number 22 is **a message from your angels** to maintain your convictions and keep an optimistic outlook and a **positive attitude** as your desires are currently being manifested for you.*

Jennifer: Oh, this is good stuff!

Amy: This is my birthday 06.22 and Brian's birthday 11.22, so it's one of my favorite numbers because it connects us.

Jennifer: Love!

Amy: This is kind of like law of attraction, right? Whatever we focus on expands. When I think about the connection I have with this particular number, I see and notice it more often.

Jennifer: Yes! It's all connected. That's the word of this chapter: connection.

Pay attention to what you're thinking about and surround yourself with it. It draws it into your existence in a really big way. Without imagination, you cannot manifest. If you can't imagine a future bigger than what you have now, you won't be able to think or feel what it would be like to have something different.

For example, my friend Olivia was on a spontaneous trip with her boyfriend a while ago. They hadn't made any hotel plans for the night and her boyfriend Chris was turning into a bit of a stress bug over it. Olivia, staying as cool as a cucumber, announces to him "we are going to meet some awesome people and befriend them. They are going to invite us to stay in their home and we'll say yes." Her boyfriend thought she was crazy, but that's exactly what happened.

They met a woman who was an artist in this small Arizona town they went to, she befriended them and took them in for the entire weekend and they are still friends to this day. In fact, we stayed there when I visited Olivia a few months ago. My friend was open to that happening and allowed it to materialize; she had the imagination to envision this option.

Amy: You have the option to ignore it, too. I like knowing that I have the power to bring magic into my life or to step back. That option grounds me; it makes the Universe seem respectful of my hesitation. That being said, I am full of gratitude that I am invited to live as magically as I want...

Jennifer: Yes, to all of that! But most importantly to that gratitude part. My friends and I are always saying, "Thanks, Uni!" (Short for Universe) it is just our fun and playful way of always acknowledging the good stuff! Gratitude is such an important step to continue receiving.

Gratitude also comes into play for experiences in our lives that we don't always love. These experiences are still things we must go through to evolve. We are always calling lessons into our life until we learn that particular lesson. These are opportunities for our growth if we are open to accepting them. It will accelerate our evolvement. It's so important to pay attention to these lessons and do the inner work.

Unfortunately, some people take things so personally that they listen to the ego and fear that tells them the people or experience is "bad," instead of looking at it like, what can I learn from this?

Amy: I think I know what you mean. I always want to learn what I'm supposed to learn so I can "graduate" to the next step in my life.

That being said, there are also times when I don't know if someone's negativity is about me or if it's about them. Sometimes they are in a negative zone and it's not directly related to me. That confusion can really get in the way of learning the lesson if you make everything about you.

Is that the ideal time to check in with your soul to receive the lesson so you don't have to keep experiencing the same thing over and over in order to "learn" it?

Jennifer: Yes, you have so many powerful experiences, and you're so open to learning all the time, I love that. But just know that there are times when you won't get it right away, but you'll understand later. Don't worry or stress about it in the moment, but trust that it will come up later and you'll come to understanding at the perfect time. In the end, all you have to do is stay open to learning and it will all work out.

Amy: I dig that. And I also like it when you say everyone you meet is for your growth or the other person's growth.

Jennifer: Yes, every single person is connected. If a person comes into your life, it is never an accident. Either you are meant to change their life in some way, they are meant to change yours, or a little of both. When you begin to come from a place of understanding this concept, your life flows so much easier. You let go of so much resistance.

Amy: I am getting better and better at putting that theory into practice. The more I feel connected to a bigger energetic experience, the less attached I am to the smaller, everyday stuff.

Jennifer: You are so good at this, Amy, you are much more aware than you give yourself credit for sometimes.

Amy: I'm good at synchronicity?

Jennifer: You're good at noticing the patterns or when answers pop up right when you need them.

Amy: It's funny you say that because I went on a walk with my boys the other day and we started talking about motorbikes. Or dirt bikes, whatever you call them; not real motorcycles. My middle son randomly asked me if he could get one. I thought that was strange since it's never come up before, but we talked about it for a while and I admitted that I didn't know a lot about the rules around permits, licenses, etcetera, for that type of motorized vehicle. I said we didn't even have anywhere they could ride them. They quickly countered that they could ride them on the neighborhood walking/bike paths, like the one on which we were currently walking.

I said, "No way, Jose! You can't ride a dirt bike here, too dangerous. And besides, I've never seen one back here in all the times we've walked or biked this route"

Jennifer: I think I know where this is going!

Amy: Ha, it's semi-predictable at this point, but at the time it made us all go silent. Right after I said "we've never seen one on the paths," a dirt bike comes out of nowhere and rips down the path ahead of us. We all stopped and looked at each other.

I said, "Well, how's that for timing?"

Jennifer: Ha! Universal timing; always right on the money.

Amy: The boys were all wound up, "like what are the odds he would drive by right now? And look, if he's doing it, we could do it." I was quick to point out that just because someone is doing something, that doesn't automatically make it permissible. He wasn't wearing a helmet, which all three boys conceded is a big No-No.

They kind of believed me at this point and seemed a little floaty by the coincidence, but then they started drilling me again for answers about dirt bikes. Finally told them I simply didn't have any experience and we'd have to ask someone who knew more about dirt bike laws. They seemed disappointed until we saw my friend round the corner with some of the children she watches during the day. They asked if she saw the dirt bike and she said yes. Then she told us her son had had a dirt bike in this same area and had gotten in a lot of trouble with police officers at various points because of all the conflicting rules around their use.

Jennifer: She was also right on time! Thanks, Uni!

Amy: Yep! That's when I couldn't help speaking out about the s-word. I told the boys this is synchronicity at its best: really fast, super concrete, and fun. I also concluded that the Universe must have wanted this conversation to be done as soon as it started because we got a lot of feedback back-to-back.

Jennifer: I love that story and I like how you look at this topic as fun. That light, playful outlook attracts the miracles and magic of synchronicity to show up.

Amy: I never take myself too seriously. I feel like most of the "magic," as you call it, that shows up in my life is a wink from the Universe, Source, or God. It makes me feel connected (there's our word again!) and seen. I don't ever feel dependent on miracles, like in a low energy, needy type of way, but I do appreciate and enjoy when moments of synchronicity happen.

For example, I often think about someone and then they reach out to me. I call these type of experiences "creepy cool" because I want to acknowledge that they are beyond normal and kind of creepy, but also really fun and cool.

Overall, it makes my life so much easier when I can simply think or feel something into existence. If I want to connect with someone, or some experience in general, I usually just think about it or speak it aloud to someone.

Jennifer: I know that you have another example for me!

Amy: Kind of. I have a running joke that if I ask aloud for something, it will happen within 24 hours, so I have to stay open and ready. I try not to get freaked out when things suddenly happen. So one example was when I told my friend that my dream was to help women share their stories, and that I'd even write their stories for them, if they couldn't write them for themselves.

Jennifer: Awwww, so sweet!

Amy: Thanks! I'm so sweet (laughs). Anyway, the next evening that same friend and I were at a meeting together. When I introduced myself to the group, I said I had recently written a book. As soon as the meeting ended, the woman leading the meeting ran up to me and said, "you have to ghostwrite my book for me. Telling my story has been on my bucket list forever. I can't write it, but I know you can." Meanwhile, my friend was walking behind her going, "Girl, you put it out into the Universe!"

My head was spinning, but I was somewhat prepared for her request since I had just been talking about it the night before. Without any more hesitation, I said I would help her. Six months later her book was published.

Jennifer: I freaking love it. Yes, yes, yes!

Amy: I wonder how Divas could start seeing and appreciating the coincidences in their lives. Should homework be to start noticing numbers? Creepy, cool timing?

Jennifer: I like those ideas and you made me reflect on all of those times when you're thinking of someone and you notice something intimately linked to them suddenly pop up in your space. Like their favorite song, an item that belongs to them, or something that *only* reminds you of that one person. Or have you ever randomly thought about someone and then they call or text you...or run into you when you're out and about?

Amy: That has definitely happened to me. I love noticing the synchronicities or, said differently, how life seems to be so synchronized sometimes. I'll say to myself, "I wonder how so-and-so is doing" and then I'll hear from them or about them without having to ask.

Jennifer: Since we are going to talk about manifesting later, I want to distinguish that synchronicity, especially the way that you just talked about it: things happening in an almost coordinated way, goes hand in hand with manifesting. But they are still different.

Amy: Manifesting feels like material possessions. Like you can manifest the ideal mate, a car, your lost wedding ring?

Jennifer: Yes, but your story about the ghostwriting client teeters on the edge between synchronicity and manifesting. On one hand it's definitely a cool story about things working out and you getting the gig you requested, but I still like it for this chapter because the timing and alignment of everything happening so quickly.

Amy: I agree; they both apply to that story because something real came out of that exchange. Sometimes I like synchronicity because I'll say I really want a plum-colored hair and suddenly I'll see ladies with that hair color everywhere. I don't get anything out of it, but it's definitely great timing.

Jennifer: Great points, but I want to keep this simple. This book is an intro conversation to all of these terms and tools, so let's make the homework pretty straight-forward.

Amy: I love me some homework!

Jennifer: You're an adorable suck-up. Let's try to get more synchronicity in our lives by learning to "see" the numbers.

Homework:

Set your phone or watch alarm to go off at 11:11 or 12:12 or 12:34. Set it for as many as you want in a day. Allow yourself to pause, look at the time, and appreciate the moment. You're just getting started. Your alignment and your openness to synchronicity is going to start a series of shifts in your life. Hold on to your Spanx, it's gonna be fun!

CHAPTER 8

Meditation &
Mindfulness

Amy: You're the first person who I've worked with who uses meditation to activate your thoughts and brain. Before you, I always thought it was just clearing your mind.

Jennifer: Oh, yeah, I love using meditation for active healing. I worked with a woman who was upset with her spouse and I told her to meditate and send positive energy and love to him. It really helped her gain some peace within their relationship.

That being said, we need to talk about how people mix up the purpose of prayer and meditation: often a prayer is form of asking; whereas meditation is about staying open to answers. People frequently say "please, please, please" in prayer mode, but never get quiet to hear the answer.

Me, of all people, should get quiet more often. My brain is a hamster wheel, and I'm always floating through tons of ideas. I try not to get tied down to every passing thought, so I will say "I'll get back to it later" to myself. I'm not saying it's easy, I'm just saying it really, really works.

Amy: I agree, writers need it, too. Before a group writing exercise, I often ask each writer to brain dump all the thoughts they have swirling around in their head. Once they "dump" for 5 minutes, they can get to the task at hand instead of endlessly channeling other stuff that isn't needed now. When we write on paper we can get it out of the mix in our brain.

Jennifer: That's good, but I just thought of something that I need to tell you.

When you spend an hour or more with people in one of your workshops, I'd really like you to help them get in touch with their inner "writer-guide." I'm thinking that particular guide would be a member of their spiritual team that can assist with writing. Do this with a quick meditation. Talk them through the visualization of energy coming through the top of their head and then going down their face, their arms, through their torso and draining all the stuff that needs to leave them so it can return to the Earth.

And then have them envision a white, clear light that is ideal for inviting their writer-guide through a clear channel. With your writers, you can have them call to their guides who can support them as they begin sharing their wisdom. Remember, your spirit team doesn't help unless you ask. This act of calling them forth should never take more than a few minutes. It doesn't have to be difficult or long and drawn out.

Something familiar you can compare it to going into surgery. Often people will pray that a surgeon has focus and success. For your part, you can call in the doctor's guides or their spiritual team and you can also extend protection over the person having the operation and call in their team of spirits, healers, or protectors. This is a great example to make it relatable for people who are warming up to the idea of asking for assistance.

Amy: I will start using that more often. I have a shorter version that I use now with grounding and breathing. I also try to use different terms for the Universe or prayer so that more people are open to trying these new techniques. A big message with this book is that we need to be more connected to others, but with meditation, and this chapter, it's more about connecting with Source.

Jennifer: I agree. It's hard to connect to one another if we can't connect to Source. One of life's challenges is to keep it real; to remember we live in the real world where life gets hectic and busy. It's all a part of learning about strength and connection to Universal energy. Not everybody needs to go off to a temple, or has time. Sometimes you need to practice quickly returning to center, or finding your inner peace, even in the midst of screaming at your children.

Amy: Agreed. I love going away and "being on the mountaintop" on retreat or even just meditating in a room alone, but my real practice comes when I'm interacting with all of the other souls I'm living with in this high-energy house.

Jennifer: I couldn't agree more. Being in true alignment with who you are is what keeps things coming to you. Our goal is to be able to stay in flow while living in this human world. The human connection walks side by side with the spiritual connection.

Amy: Is this what people mean when they refer to Mindfulness?

Jennifer: Absolutely, this is an extension of meditation. It's like meditation in action. You can be mindful with anything. For example, it is important to be mindful of your decisions and people you attract in your life.

One of the most important lessons I learned on this subject is; I don't have to entangle myself with everyone I encounter. I tell myself, Jennifer, you do not have to support *everybody*. I have to consciously acknowledge this now because I used to feel like I had to help everyone who asked and it exhausted me mentally and energetically. I wasn't being mindful; actually that's pretty mindless. Just doing, doing, doing, without bring awareness to the interaction.

To recap: when you meet someone, you want to have an energetic match so that the exchange is mutually beneficial. Bring awareness to your togetherness *right away*. When the vibration created in the relationship is in harmony, growth can happen and you won't feel depleted.

Amy: I think that is also important for workplaces; you are either connected or not.

Jennifer: And that's why most harmonious relationships at work make your efforts feel so efficient. You are both aware and vibing on a high level.

Amy: If mindfulness in new relationships or at work is useful...what about in marriage or romantic relationships?

Jennifer: Oh, girl. I'm so glad you asked! Another cool way to use meditative techniques is during sex!

Amy: Whoa, you just jumped right to sex, didn't you?

Jennifer: Ha! Sorry, not sorry. Meditation while having sex is so powerful because you can get into a totally different space. For example, if you notice your mind wandering, you can acknowledge those thoughts and release them. Simply tell your random thoughts that you will connect with them later. Instead, focus on your lady parts and pull all energy to the area you want to enhance.

Amy: I can do that!

Jennifer: Another fun tip: the fastest way to manifest is during orgasm. When you bring the orgasm back into your energy versus releasing it out of your energy you create an amazing energy vortex. My friend thinks that writing out affirmations is the best. I lovingly disagree with her and say that writing things doesn't work for me. Orgasms, though? Works every time!

Another point to make, not orgasm-related (sorry): there is never just one way to get shifts in your life. For me, when I stay in alignment, I find that I can manifest with ease. It's all about getting out of a slump and back to a space that feels good. I always say, "a negative breeds a negative."

However, when you don't acknowledge the negative you are feeling, it breeds like rabbits. You must validate when you are feeling negative and work with it and then work it out. Don't ignore real emotional pain and simply replace it with a positive thought. That is not honoring your feelings and it is not alignment. Remember everything, including the pain, is a lesson.

Amy: I remember hearing you say that pain is a lesson *disguised* as reality. It's not really real, it's valuable experience, but it can be transcended. I visualize that as stepping away from the "reality" of the hurt and stepping towards a deeper understanding that feels loving and safe. This idea is so comforting to me.

Heavy stuff; learning can sometimes be hard. It's not always sunshine and orgasms!

Jennifer: Unfortunately, that's true. (laughs) The main idea in this chapter is to stay connected to Source and to those who are a high energy match for you. Ultimately our goal is to try to maintain mindfulness so we can understand the situation as it is, not as what we want it to be.

Amy: Maintaining mindfulness feels so neutral. Staying in a space of neutrality makes me feel peaceful.

Jennifer: Good! You don't have to get swept up and emotionally tossed about. Neutrality is a great way to describe that Zen state of being.

Amy: Have you ever felt like you were in a place where it would be impossible to meditate? What would be a worst case scenario?

Jennifer: Impossible? I can't think of anywhere that you *couldn't* meditate. I was recently in an MRI machine meditating, if you can believe that. Those things are sooo loud! It's pretty horrible and I even had a hockey-type mask over my face and earplugs *and* headphones blocking some out the noise. I had to take out my nose-ring for the scan and my nose started itching where I had taken it out... which made a sneeze came up. I knew if I sneezed I was going to smash not only my face against the mask, but the mask against the lid of the machine I was in. I had no other choice, so I left my body and didn't worry about human Jennifer sneezing. I felt myself float up and away from that uncomfortable body for the rest of the procedure. That was a real lesson for me. I want everyone to understand now: you are separate from your body. Meditation is allowing yourself to be more in your spirit than in your body.

Amy: That's perfect. We've all heard people who have been in traumatic situations talk about how it felt like they left their body. It's a real phenomenon that we don't discuss very often, but we all have a sense of understanding when we hear about it. I get some strange sense of comfort knowing that, again, I have the power to float away. And I have the power to return intact.

Jennifer: Yes, you do! Whether it's in the workplace, during sex, or in an uncomfortable situation, you are always in control.

Amy: This may seem random, but I just remembered that I love my detox bath for meditating, too. You taught me how to do that. Remember? Cup of baking soda, cup of Epsom or Dead Sea salt, and a few shakes of any essential oil.

Jennifer: Of course! You've got to make the water as HOT as you can handle! You need to sweat while you're in the tub.

Amy: I never make plans for after a detox bath. It wipes me out; I'm always ridiculously relaxed. I think every single time I almost immediately zonk out.

Jennifer: Nothing better than post-detox sleep!

Amy: Alright, it's homework time. What should we work on now? Detox baths for everyone!

Jennifer: Of course!! I'm going to add a couple of other things to try, too!

Homework:

Detox Bath Directions: Run a bath as hot as you can tolerate. Add 1-2 cups of Epsom Salt or Sea Salt depending on how big your tub is. Add same amount of baking soda. Pour in around 1 tablespoon of unpasteurized Apple Cider vinegar. Add several drops of Lavender essential oil. Essential oils are optional, but nice for relaxing. Stay in minimum of 20 minutes with any doors or curtains closed to contain everything.

When draining the tub set the intention that any negativity you release goes down the drain and returns to Mother Earth to transmute.

AND / OR

Calling In Your Guides: Whatever you're working on that uses your creativity or talent, practice calling in your helper guides for that particular area to assist you. Like the examples in this chapter of the doctors and writer guides. Watch the shift in what you are able to do and what comes to you.

AND / OR

Journal about two people who are no longer in your life. Write about how one of them changed your life. Then write about how the other person was changed by you. Include as much detail as you can about these experiences. You will be so surprised what comes up!

CHAPTER 9

Intuition

Amy: What does it mean to be psychic?

Jennifer: Hmmm. I have mixed feelings. I feel like psychic is not as powerful a word as it used to be. One reason is it used to be thought of as "rare" when, now more and more people are stepping into their power in this specific way. Another (unfortunate) reason is because a lot of frauds have popped up all over calling themselves psychics and taking advantage of people.

Okay, so what does it mean to be psychic? When you have insight, you can "see into" other's lives or into a future event. For some they can see into their own life and their future, but, for the most part, people can see into the lives of others' lives much more than their own.

9 times out of 10 I can see for others what they can't see for themselves. I can tap into their inner compass. Being psychic or intuitive used to be an inaccessible

term, but now it's something that applies to so many of us. Everybody has a gift and the potential to be very intuitive, but most people don't even try.

Amy: I want to try! What should I do?

Jennifer: Girl, you already do it! When you tell me thoughts or images you "see" about me when we talk, you're tapping into your intuition. You are so open to messages that they present themselves to you easily.

Amy: Oh, I didn't really think about that being psychic. I really feel tuned in when I'm helping people write their book. I always get distinct ideas about what they should do with their story. I don't "think" about it, the ideas just bubble up or pop up as they talk.

Jennifer: Exactly! You are allowing that wisdom or insight to come through you for your writing clients. You also channel when you write!! Channeling, psychic, different words; same thing!

Amy: It seems like a pretty specific niche for me, though. You, on the other hand, get all types of information for people. Do you have to ask yourself, or Spirit, for a specific message?

Jennifer: Yes, remember we talked about that with tarot cards? I do that with any message. I get myself in a space where I am in vibration with a person and I can hear the message that is meant for them.

Amy: That sounds like a delicate process. I wonder if your abilities or intuition can come and go.

Jennifer: They can be neglected, that's for sure. My daughter, Emma, has a gift that shows up during her downtime. Right now she's so busy that there doesn't seem to be any space for her intuition. When she was younger she had more time to let those gifts come through. When we moved to a small town years ago, it was winter and she didn't know anyone. She had lots of downtime and lots of intuitive experiences. Every time she told me something, I was like, whoa! She isn't as open, in every sense, any more. That could change though.

Amy: I don't think you felt as connected to your intuition after AJ died. I remember you telling me how detached you felt during periods of time while you grieved. That being said, I also remember how you experienced the floodgates opening after you had a powerful session with *your* intuitive healers.

Jennifer: Oh my gosh, it was crazy.

Amy: I know you mentioned it already, but I want to remind all the super "tough, independent" Divas out there that we all need healing from time to time. I think it's important for them to remember that healers go to healers.

Jennifer: I'm a huge fan of receiving healing for myself. As crazy as it sounds, it takes me a long time to realize I need healing sometimes. Fortunately, my spirit guides will nudge me or my friends, who work on me, will straight up call me and tell me I need to come in for a session.

Amy: So even though we can do a lot on our own, we still need to get worked on by people who are gifted at healing?

Jennifer: Yes, no question about it.

Amy: On the flip side, you and I have talked about how people can become dependent on their psychics sometimes. You hear about people who won't make a decision without consulting them.

I wonder if readers should use all the tools we've talked about so far just like how you *should* use a doctor or psychiatrist or even medicine: sometimes you need them when you're not doing well. They can help to get you back to 100% healthy, but you never want to be dependent on them.

Jennifer: I agree. You can be a healthy person in general and still need to go to the doctor or take a medicine from time to time. We all need to go in for certain tests and bloodwork. It's key to know ourselves so we know when to get that check-up or that reboot.

Amy: I guess this is part of developing our intuition. We have to learn when we can do things on our own versus when we need to get additional help.

Jennifer: I have some guided audio supports that I'm developing in conjunction with this book for online, but many readers may be guided to start develop a relationship with a variety of healers directly. It would be ideal if they could start to identify like-minded people and/or professionals who can support the lessons that they've learned here. Meanwhile, we all have an opportunity to become comfortable working on our own inner guidance

Amy: All of that sounds great. I hope no one feels overwhelmed by too many tools. When in doubt, Divas, pick one. Personally, I like the idea that we can develop our sense of intuition which can steer us to the future we want.

Jennifer: Of course! In any situation you can check-in and ask: does this feel "right" or does this feel "true"? This is a really easy first step to aligning with your guidance. We have a lot of homework assignments for our overachieving ladies. Let's see how they do.

Homework:

A great way to work with your intuition is to keep a log of your dreams and interpret them. Look for the hidden meanings and messages. The more you write your dreams down, the more that will come to you. Keep a notebook or recording device next to your bed. Not everyone wants to write upon waking up, so recording what you remember in your best morning voice is good, too! I also like to send myself texts!

AND / OR

Do something that you are drawn to do that is creative. Creativity really brings our intuition to the forefront and puts a spotlight on it. Focus on whatever "creativity" means to you, not to anyone else.

AND / OR

When taking a shower don't just rush through it. Allow the water to run over you and don't focus on anything other than just relaxing. Showers are one of the best places to get intuitive insights.

CHAPTER 10

Supporting Energy in Relationships

Amy: I definitely notice an energy connection in relationships; especially with Brian. What do I need to know to be a better spouse and have a "stronger" marriage?

Jennifer: This is a great conversation around romantic relationships. So often we come to others with the energy and perspective *we* have instead of trying to meet with them at the energy level or perspective *they* have.

Amy: I get that...I do. But it's easier said than done.

Jennifer: I realize that, but this is too important not to try. You can dump the negative feelings with your partner. It's important to be able to vent and to recognize that those low-energy feelings are valid.

Amy: I get that. We all want to be heard and feel like we're not crazy for being upset.

Jennifer: You want empathy in your relationship; for your partner to feel what you're feeling and vice versa, but you don't want too much negativity. Therefore, you want to avoid embracing low-energy projections. You can do this when you both move beyond the perception that if something is bad it always has to stay bad. Instead, you can choose to work together to feel positive. If you come from a place of love and happiness, you won't focus on the bad aspects of your situation.

After a necessary rant, you want to align your energy with your partner and lift each other up. The goal is to move beyond the negativity, even if it takes a little while.

Amy: I feel like I should share a quick story even though it makes me look bad.

Jennifer: Do it!

Amy: My friend was telling me about a frustrating situation she got into with a mutual friend. Their kids were having trouble getting along and my friend felt that our mutual friend never addressed the bullying behavior her daughter exhibited that really impacted all of the kids.

Instead our mutual friend would defend her daughter's harmful behavior to the detriment of other children.

It was definitely a sticky situation and, without thinking, I jumped in and added to the negativity of the conversation. I agreed that the other mom was totally enabling her daughter's tyrannical ways. It was a pretty judge-y conversation. When we got off the phone I felt so icky. I instantly knew I had energetically played it all wrong.

Jennifer: Explain a little more. I like where this is going.

Amy: Well, I had a choice when she started complaining about our friend. I could have just held the space for her to vent and then supported her as she came to her own healing conclusions, but I didn't do that. In a sense, I handed her a mic and joined her onstage and contributed my own rant. We were two gals piling up the negativity higher and higher.

Jennifer: This is a great example of a low energy conversation. You were trying to find areas where you agreed and had common beliefs, but it was bringing you both down. That's why you felt "icky" afterwards. No one stepped up to lead the healing.

Amy: I could tell I messed up as soon as we hung up. Uggh.

Jennifer: This happens in arguments, too. 9 times out of 10 the person who has the most power doesn't want that much responsibility, instead of picking one house or another, the people involved need to build a whole new house together.

Amy: You lost me. We are using a lot of metaphors today, by the way.

Jennifer: Sorry, not sorry. I love metaphors! The house comparison is showing how in an argument there are people who are trying to persuade you to agree with them, come over to their perspective; to get you to move from your "house" to their "house."

Amy: Oh, I think I understand. It almost sounds like the current situation or perspective isn't good enough so, together, they need to create a "new normal" together instead of convincing one person to completely abandon their beliefs and embrace all of your beliefs.

Jennifer: Yep. That type of compromise, if you can even call it that, never makes either party feel great.

Amy: I agree, co-creating always feels magical, whereas, convincing someone to your side...or being convinced, always feel like someone loses in the transaction.

Jennifer: Co-creating IS magic. That's a great way to support the energy in a relationship, too.

Amy: Plus, you'll always have that creation that you and the other person made together. It energetically bonds you together.

Jennifer: You're so right, Amy, but you just made me think of something. We need to be careful how we co-create and who we do it with. Things can get pretty messy, pretty quickly if we're not making conscious choices.

Amy: That sounded way dirtier than I think you meant it. Actually it reminds me of the unprotected sex analogy from the first chapter.

Jennifer: I do sound dirty! While I like that analogy for working with an energy healer, here's an analogy that may help when we're focusing on co-creating with someone: Sometimes we get excited and start adding too many different colors to our life's painting. We think all these "colors" will result a new beautiful color or image, but it ends up the color of shit. We need to make more conscious choices.

Amy: So just because you can work with someone and engage in a relationship, any kind of relationship, that doesn't mean you necessarily should?

Jennifer: You got it.

Amy: And the relationships we definitely want to be in? What should we do if it's starting to feel like a messy painting?

Jennifer: That usually happens when there is a power struggle and your trying to control one another. Or one person is trying to control and the other one is resisting.

Amy: Sounds like some of the disagreements, or power struggles, that Brian and I have.

Jennifer: If you are trying to get him to be like you, or vice versa, you could end up with a messy painting. You two can slip from co-creating to power struggle.

Amy: Yep, that has happened. When he doesn't engage in the creation stuff, I kind of just become the decider.

Jennifer: When you have an argument or high-risk conversation, it's high risk to the person who will lose their power or voice, and then one person dominates while the other person energetically retreats.

Amy: I win a lot of arguments or discussions under those circumstances. He retreats and I get the win and it feels... blah.

Jennifer: It's a perceived win. We win because we don't have to hear about ourselves. Most of us don't want to hear those things so we railroad the person who *could* tell us until they stop coming for us.

Amy: I don't want that though. I want him to be engaged. I want B to fight for himself, to fight for us.

Jennifer: Not fight, find his voice so he can speak openly in a safe space. You need to show him that you want his opinion and you want him to feel valued. You can even say to him, "I want your voice to be important and for mine to be equally important."

Amy: I want to say that to him...like now. As I'm thinking about all of this, I also wonder if he won't "fight" with me or for us is because fighting always equals losing. At least that was his experience from childhood. He's risk=averse because he doesn't wat to lose the love, happiness, etc. he has now.

Jennifer: Absolutely. And doesn't' that make sense? Just by recognizing his perspective you're helping co-create a better future together.

Here's one way you can navigate an impasse in your marriage. Instead of escalating it to the level of a "fight," keep it a conversation. If you say something that seems to make him flinch or bristle, instead of rolling your eyes or asking "what's wrong now?" say, "I feel like what I just said doesn't resonate with you." It keeps things loving and honest without triggering him further.

Amy: I can do that.

Jennifer: That would be so much better than "what are you mad about now?" which amps up the conflict and shuts him down.

Amy: I really, really get that.

Jennifer: You can start doing that during your interactions today.

Amy: And I will. I feel a shift in my perception just thinking about how I can respond differently

Jennifer: Or even changing your expectations around what it means to be in conversation with him.

Amy: Yes, I see how we think differently and communicate differently, but that's definitely not a bad thing.

Jennifer: Not at all! But to get back to expectations, for him, expectations lead to disappointment because he's experienced that in the past.

Amy: I wonder if that's why we're a couple; we balance each other out or we heal each other's wounds.

Jennifer: No doubt. These types of relationships can be the greatest pairs or end up very strained. There's a lot of work that needs to be done to be able heal and grow together.

Wanting what you never had is normal, but it's hard to accept the new normal if you co-created something imbalanced growing up.

Amy: It forces you to revisit the past as you navigate the present. I don't love taking him back to those childhood feelings. Or even back to times in our marriage where I feel like he shut down. I still remember how lonely it was when I found out I had my second miscarriage because he didn't really process with me.

Jennifer: It's hard to go through that, but sharing about that experience and how you felt and asking how he felt could be really helpful now.

Amy: Hmmm. I'm going to ask him. I think you're right it, it feels more neutral now.

Jennifer: His insights will be refreshing, for both of you. You're not trying to rewrite the past, by the way.

Amy: Hmm, I'm a little nervous that he'll think I'm being weird bringing up something from 13 years ago, but I'm willing to try. I like the idea that we're not rewriting the past, so there's no reason for debating or arguing, just understanding.

Jennifer: Exactly. I'm excited to hear how it goes. Are you ready for another relationship analogy?

Amy: Yes, please!

Jennifer: This one is about trees. Sometimes we need to plant a new family tree next to the old family tree. Together we can create a new family dynamic and new story.

For example, my family can disconnect in an instant. I was daddy's little girl until age 15 when I went against him. I can still remember when he said, "take a good look at me for your book of memories, you'll never see me again."

And I never did, as you know he died when I was 16.

Amy: I didn't realize you were two were estranged when he passed away.

Jennifer: Yes, it's so painful and confusing. His brother did the same thing with his kids. My uncle was so disconnected from his own kids until, ironically, he met my oldest son as a toddler. That encounter then led to him watching his great-granddaughter, which ultimately led to a lot of healing. Unfortunately, he didn't live too many years after that.

Just to give you some context for the dynamics in my family, (brace yourself) my grandfather slept with his son's wife after they divorced. There was even talk of my dad fathering my cousin, a few other "illegitimate children," grudge-holding like no other, and disowning children. My family is so dysfunctional and damaged. People in my family aren't even sure who their biological parents are because of the dysfunctional relationships.

Amy: This makes my heart ache.

Jennifer: The good news is my mom tells me how my brother and I are breaking the cycle. We are creating new family norms.

Amy: I love the idea of new, happier, norms.

Jennifer: I have been learning and growing out of the dysfunction, but I understand now that we can't be pushed. Shifts and healing have to happen in their own time. It's been a long road for me to feel whole and good and I've had so many teachers along the way.

One of the biggest things I know now is that you have a choice to heal. You can tell me that I'm hurting you or disappointing you, and I can decide that I want to do something about it or not. It all comes down to deciding how I want our relationship to develop, heal, or even dissolve.

Amy: I see that with Brian, too. He hates the word "expectation" and I think that concept comes up a lot when you're in a family or long-term relationship.

Jennifer: When B hears someone talk about an "expectation" he automatically assumes he'll disappoint someone.

For him, or anyone who expresses resistance to engaging, I'd ask, "How would I feel right now if I was in their shoes?" I always try to come from where they live versus where I live. People are always trying to get others to do things their way instead of trying see things from a different perspective.

Amy: I'm guilty of that. I try to understand from my perspective, not necessarily from their perspective.

Jennifer: We all want to help, it's just that our attempts to help aren't always helpful. After AJ's death, people's focus was for me to be "back to normal" so when I laughed they would be relieved. It would make *them* feel good. On some level, we all are trying to feel good.

Amy: We want to feel helpful, but I doubt anyone consciously wants to make someone feel bad in that process.

Jennifer: Agreed, that's why consciousness is so important. Around this same time, my brother was upset with me because I wasn't calling my mom. It was making her "feel bad" that I wasn't reaching out to her. While I totally get that, I didn't want to talk to anyone at that point. Eventually I asked my brother, "does that mean I have to feel bad and do something I don't want to do so that mom can feel good?" I think he kind of understood my point of view after that.

I can't do things the way other people do it. I never properly grieved my father's death, or saw anyone around me grieving him either, which meant I had no example for grieving the death of my friend. I had to figure out how to handle it on my own.

I love all the people in my life, but I ultimately decided to put myself first. People have to create space for themselves and find their own path.

Amy: I agree. Even though it feels selfish, we have to address our needs before we entangle ourselves with others.

I think it's hard sometimes to find the balance between what you want to do and what's good for the energy of the relationship.

Jennifer: Boundaries are key in that regard. All balanced relationships have established boundaries where you don't have to always do what the other person wants you to.

Amy: We see how we could do that in all relationships, with friends, neighbors, co-workers, etc. First establish boundaries that feel good and *then* make decisions that keep the energy circulating in a positive, productive way.

Jennifer: For sure. And remember: your way of living, being raised, etc. is different from others' experiences. Moving forward I predict women are going to build a new foundation or a new normal, collectively. Building a house *together* is so important. An energizing relationship is a creation that you build together. You don't build a house separately or with one perspective; it must be done together. Co-creation is the key.

Amy: You've given me a lot to think about. There are several words or ideas that I want to let go of: winning, fighting, and compromise. On the flip side, I'd like to start thinking of everything in terms co-creation within the boundaries of the relationship.

Jennifer: That could lead to a great homework assignment after this chapter.

Amy: I bet it has something to do with our perception of relationships.

Jennifer: We can all benefit from doing a little self-evaluation on our relationships.

Amy: Beyond our romantic partnerships?

Jennifer: Yes, I think it would be great to reflect on how we show up in all of the major relationships of our life. Even work relationships can be analyzed.

Amy: I'm excited! I want to have smoother, more supportive relationships moving forward and I know that I need to raise my consciousness big time.

Jennifer: Great! Here's your chance!

Homework:

When I say "relationship," what is the first relationship in your life that comes to mind immediately? This does not have to be romantic.

Write down YOUR behaviors that you are really proud of in this relationship and the ones that you are not so proud of. Try to come up with 5 for each.

Now flip perspectives with that person, write the list of what THEY are proud of and not so proud of in THEIR behaviors. (use your imagination)

When you finish circle the similarities and box the differences.

Now you are going to write a letter to them (You do NOT have to give it to them)

Write whatever comes to mind of the experiences you have had, what you love, what you wish were different. How you plan to move forward with your new awareness, etc.

When you finish take a lighter or match and burn it in a safe place. Release it and allow the energy to move!

CHAPTER 11

Manifesting Stuff

Amy: I love the idea that we have the power to connect with others, to find balance within ourselves, and to develop our intuition. Oh, and synchronicity. That's a similar tool to what we're going to talk about now. I have to think that manifesting stuff is just another aspect of all these universal skills.

Jennifer: Absolutely, I'm so glad you brought this up because I think people have heard a lot about the law of attraction and we should make the link from what we've discussed in earlier chapters to manifestation in everyday life.

Amy: It's so fun; you know, getting stuff.

Jennifer: You are a master manifestor, Amy. I'm always like, "Girl, you are in the vortex!"

Amy: I love it when you tell me that. It forces me to take stock of how quickly blessings come into to my life.

When you announce that I'm living in the vortex, which I take to mean I'm in flow and aligned with abundant experiences...

Jennifer: Yes! Exactly!

Amy: ...it just makes me amp up my gratitude. That's one of the best ways to "stay blessed;" stay in constant gratitude. I'm sure our readers have heard that "what you focus on expands" which I have found completely true whether it's me complimenting my kids' loving behavior (spoiler: they end up being more and more loving after I tell them that) or me feeling complete appreciation for the Universe/God/Spirit giving me the perfect people and circumstances to aid in my spiritual growth. I have faith because I have faith.

Jennifer: Huh? I'm going to need a little more explanation on that last point.

Amy: I didn't mean to get all vague, but I feel like my faith has deepened the more that I've believed everything is happening for my greatest good. I also know that this life is a playground and we are allowed to play however we want. I'm not greedy, but I like experiencing success.

I know that I'm allowed to be happy, so I experience a lot of happiness. I like the idea of the Earth as a playground. My soul feels very light-hearted within that construct. I also think that vibe makes manifesting easier, right?

Jennifer: Heck, yeah!

Amy: So my faith continuously feeds my faith and *that* allows me to be open to receiving.

Jennifer: That is a huge part of manifesting, actually. People forget to *allow* the thing that they want into their lives.

Amy: And so they squash it just as it's about to become a reality? I've seen so many people do that. It's hard to watch people give up right when things are about to become magically awesome.

Jennifer: I agree, but allowing blessings and feeling worthy of abundance are two very challenging concepts.

Amy: People are talking about worthiness all the time now. Especially women.

Jennifer: Because so many women are still trying to get there; they know they want to be happy, but it seems strange to be required to "allow" it. A lot of independent Divas don't know how to do that.

Amy: It's like accepting any kind of help. I used to be resistant to asking or accepting help because I was always taught not to impose on others. I love helping people, though. I like knowing what people need and then specifically giving them what I can without angst or feelings of attachment. Sometimes it's a hug, sometimes it's just holding the space for them so they can be happy or sad without judgement.

Jennifer: So do you let people help you now?

Amy: Yes. I'm getting better, anyway. There was a tipping point when I let a new friend come over to my house to give me emergency acupuncture when I messed up my neck. I had to give her my address because she hadn't been to my house before. I can still remember how I was *so* resistant to receiving her help. She kept pushing me, so I finally said okay and told her where I lived.

Jennifer: I remember this story. Is this when you couldn't move your head?

Amy: Yes, I don't know what I did, but it was getting worse and worse throughout the day. Once she came over I gave up any resistance that I previously had and just relaxed in her care. I wanted to feel better and I trusted that she knew how to do that. She totally numbed out the pain and taught me ways to continue healing myself with turmeric tea.

Jennifer: Please tell me you're getting all the parallels between this story and how manifesting works!

Amy: Uh, my friend is like the Universe and you need to ask *and* allow for what you need?

Jennifer: Ding, ding, ding. We have a winner!

Amy: Ha, I hadn't thought about how perfectly that syncs up with manifesting. I could've resisted her all day long. But I'm so glad I didn't. It felt good to be healthy and whole again. It also led to a wonderful friendship.

Jennifer: Manifesting what you want is simply articulating to yourself, and therefore, the Universe, what you want or need.

Amy: So be careful what you wish for! Getting what we want can sometimes come in interesting packaging.

Jennifer: So true! Manifesting with precision is super important. It reminds me of when my Jackson said he wanted a farmhouse, and we sure found one to look at. We went and looked at this cool farmhouse that was for sale. We were so excited to see it and from a distance it seemed perfect. It was beautiful and on a great stretch of land, but when we got closer we saw the paint was all chipped off the outside. When we got inside, it was a hot mess. Wires were everywhere, nothing finished. The washer was in the kitchen, but there were no outlets. My daughter turned to him and said, "You forgot to mention that you wanted a *nice* farmhouse. This place is a dump!"

Amy: Ha! That reminds me of when I said I want to attract people who are ready to write their first book and need my help. I remember saying: I don't want to go searching for them, I want them to find me and ask for help.

Jennifer: And you totally got that.

Amy: Uh, yeah. I was so excited how random people were showing up asking for help.

Jennifer: Yeah they were!

Amy: And with no money.

Jennifer: Hahaha! Just like Jackson and that ratty farmhouse!

Amy: So...I went back to the drawing board and asked with precision: I want to work with people who are ready to write their first book and will easily and joyfully pay my fees.

Jennifer: Better...

Amy: And to make a long story short, I got that, too. Now I realize that I want to attract women only and, specifically, women who are like me. I hesitated on the specificity for a while, but I'm kind of over it now.

Jennifer: What do you mean? You didn't want to be too specific? You have to be specific! Otherwise you'll bring all sorts of stuff into your life. People do that all the time, "I want a man because I'm tired of being alone." Then they get the deadbeat guy who doesn't do anything. What if they had asked for someone who loved them for who they were and helped them grow spiritually?

Amy: I love that, but that "growing" stuff is interesting, too. Going from a secure teaching job to becoming a full-time entrepreneur has taught me that growing usually means being uncomfortable. Growing spiritually and growing as a person with my husband has meant a lot of trying and failing and trying again. All I'm saying is if readers ask the Universe for a partner who helps them grow, they are asking for shifts to happen and sometimes shifts feel like shit.

Jennifer: Ha! I agree a million percent! But do you regret becoming an entrepreneur? Shitty shifts and all?

Amy: No way, but based on conversations I've had, or just my general observations, it seems like some people don't like being rejected. And rejections are a part of growing and learning a new business.

Jennifer: Get outta town, people don't like being rejected?!

Amy: I know, it's crazy! (laughs) I don't "like" it, but I've become so detached from the outcome of things; well, at least the details, that rejection just feels like part of the process. I'm never going to articulate that you "have to be rejected" because that seems to low energy, but I will say that rejection is a gift. It teaches you to do your best and detach from the outcome. That is actually all faith is... you do the work and then let go and let God (or Universe, Spirit, Allah, Gaia, etc.).

Jennifer: Another way to look at it is to realize when something doesn't work out the way you expected or hoped, it's not bad. Actually, it's as it should be. Each member of the interaction had the exchange that they were meant to have. You can move forward knowing that you showed up and did your part. Which circles back around to what you were saying about detachment: you can be present without smothering the situation with your expectations.

Amy: There is so much relief in just letting things be. I wish women could do that more. I wish *I* could do that more; especially as a mother and wife.

Jennifer: We are a work in progress, momma!

Homework:

Play your favorite music while visualizing what you want. Get your vibration as high as possible. Allow yourself to let go of any negativity you may be holding onto by dancing, screaming, or singing. Remember that manifesting is also highly aligned with the euphoric state of orgasm. Give it a try!

AND / OR

If your visual, create a vision board with images of whatever lights you up.

AND / OR

If you are creative in general, think about what you want more in your life as you are in the midst of your creative practice.

AND / OR

Finally, try listening to affirmations and then write some out without strain or concentration. Calmly and with loving heart, write positive statements that make you feel good.

CHAPTER 12

Connections to Everything

Amy: What's the most important lesson of this book?

Jennifer: Most important lesson? Being connected. Yes, being connected is so important. The acceptance of "what is" is so important. We are looking at people thinking and changing in new ways; shifts are happening everywhere. Everywhere! The whole planet is shifting, like even bigger than the planet. Arrgh, what's the word.

Amy: Hmmm, is it a celestial shift, a shift from the cosmos?

Jennifer: Yes! We are seeing mass consciousness go in two directions. Just like in global politics or even the American Presidential election. There are huge shifts happening and we need to remember that despite the choice to move forward in one direction versus another, we are all deeply, deeply connected.

Amy: People talk flippantly about social media, but I

feel a shift when I use Facebook or any other platform in a meaningful way. I can emotionally change when I connect with someone through a video or even a written post. I totally get that posts can be negative and low vibration, but I tend to not go down those rabbit holes. They're pretty clearly marked, if you know what I mean.

Jennifer: I definitely know what you mean, but I think the path to low vibe, low energy, or negative interactions is almost always pretty easy to see, don't you? You don't have to be psychic to see that some relationships, on social media or in-person are going to be toxic. Am I right? I don't want to assume anything.

Amy: No, I agree. Many people would admit that bad interactions rarely come out of nowhere. There is usually a series of events that contribute toward a stinky exchange. But that only reinforces the idea of this last chapter and the main idea of the book: everything is connected.

Jennifer: I also want to emphasis that people need to remember what they can already do. We are powerful beyond belief and we can accelerate all of the shifts that are already happening around the world. It's so cool that I just can't stand it!

Amy: Every time I hear that it's a very important time to live, I kind of roll my eyes. Like the ego in each of us has to think that this time, or our lives, is simply the best there ever was. But then I think about what you said to me "off the record" the other day: what if we're all correct? What if everybody was right about everything? Our understanding that we are important and our god is great may actually be right and 200 years ago their spiritual evolution and their god was right. What if everyone is right?

Jennifer: Yessssss! I'm so glad you remembered that. It really came to me out of nowhere and now I'm wondering if that's the whole point. If you want the spiritual connection to all things, all experiences, and all beings... you totally can. The celestial shifts that have been happening have allowed things to change. We are getting closer and closer to a limitless existence. Space and time have been bridged by countless technologies and now we are moving to a presence that is not defined by the limits of space and time.

Amy: Eeek, that's awesome and scary and wonderful and eeek! I hate to bring up Facebook again, but I really feel like I can be in the moment with someone even years after their posted experience happened. I bridge space and time with that energetic connection. And, it should be noted, that almost all of my clients come from Facebook. I've made deep and meaningful relationships with people I've never physically touched. Our connections would probably never have materialized before Facebook; it's such a unique global resource.

Jennifer: You know you and I haven't physically touched...yet!

Amy: Heavens to Betsy, you're right! I forget about that sometimes.

Jennifer: No doubt about it, human connection has changed in ways that are still disorienting. Some folks think it's strange to be friends with someone you haven't been in the same room with...

Amy: ...and shared some air with.

Jennifer: Yes, exactly, but I think it's becoming more normalized.

Amy: And to be crystal clear, neither one of us is saying every online interaction is awesome. I'm just saying it *can* be.

Jennifer: Oh hell no! It's not always wonderful. For millions of people it's a way to amplify their pain. The online world can also feel like someone held a megaphone up to the mouths of lots of crazy people. There's a lot pain in search of healing and we should protect ourselves online just like we do when we walk through Walmart. We do not have to absorb other people's pain.

Amy: Gotta get in our protective egg bubble thingy.

Jennifer: Yes, please. Divas, please don't forget to fasten your energetic force field *before* you interact with others. Whether it's in-person or online. And please make sure your chair is in its upright position.

Amy: You're silly.

Jennifer: It's true.

Amy: Now back to insights...what is the final word on connection?

Jennifer: I want to go back to that bridge idea you said earlier.

Amy: Remind me, what did I say about bridges?

Jennifer: Not the noun "bridge," the verb. You said, "I bridge space and time with that energetic connection." Can you see how you are the bridge between the past and your destiny?

Amy: Not really. My past and my destiny?

Jennifer: No, *the* past and your destiny.

Amy: The past. As in what happened earlier in our lives, in human existence, in our past lives?

Jennifer: Yes.

Amy: I'm the bridge?

Jennifer: Yes.

Amy: I'm a bridge? Bridges act as a connection. Love this guessing game, by the way.

Jennifer: Me, too. Keep going.

Amy: I'm a bridge because my life, my experiences, are connecting what has come before me, the past, to what is coming next, which is my destiny.

Jennifer: Oh, nice! Good job.

Amy: That makes me feel like a part of something ever growing and changing.

Jennifer: So you feel your connection to all things- energy, life, space, time, and the future?

Amy: Actually, I do. I really do.

Jennifer: You have had the opportunity to have these understandings for all of eternity. You, me, all the Divas reading this...are so powerful. We have a connection to Source energy and that's why religion has been so instrumental in our evolving existence. We have wisdom and understanding beyond our comprehension. So much wisdom that we scare ourselves and make rules to live smaller and safer. We don't want to be too big and fabulous. We don't want to shine too brightly because that could be too much power to wield. That's why we demand that our leaders or our religions take that power and make decisions and rules for us. That much power can make our connections too intense.

Amy: That reminds me of Marianne Williamson's famous line, "our deepest fear is not that we are inadequate, but we are powerful beyond measure." But that's why people read her books, and this book. To reconnect with the knowing. The power.

I think.

They may have been tricked into reading this book. This book does look quite fem-friendly.

Jennifer: True, but if they got this far...

Amy: Yeah, if you've read this far, you must feel comfortable with the discomfort of being powerful.

Jennifer: And ready to raise your consciousness around your life's purpose.

Amy: I feel like the greatest resources we have are the tools you went over in this book. I have so much more clarity around soul contracts and how relationships show up in my life. I really feel a peace around my internal balance after our chakra and crystal talk. Just everything. All the tools are so important to have in our general understanding as we move forward in this new paradigm.

Jennifer: Oh, yes, they are part of the vocabulary that we need as we move engage in this global conversation.

Raising our intuition is critical to mass consciousness.

Amy: Which is, again, all about connection. So the connection to all things and the power to create the existence you want...

Jennifer: ...that's the lesson. That's what all the tools like soul contracts, meditation, synchronicity, and the others are for. They are all available to enhance your connection *and* your power.

Amy: I feel like I want to say "eeek" again.

Jennifer: You can. It's kind of a big deal.

Amy: Eeek.

Jennifer: People need to remember what they can already do. That's it.

Amy: I love that more than I can say. "We need to remember what we can already do." Goosebumps.

Jennifer: It's a choice. A good choice, but we have to make the decision to be powerful with awareness that we are connected to one another. To everything everywhere.

Amy: Amen.

Jennifer: Reconnecting to our wisdom means connecting to the source of all life and simply remembering.

Amy: That makes me feel like I'm in the vortex. I receive that message with ease and flow. It doesn't feel scary and I don't feel dependent on you or anyone else to help me feel aligned with my purpose. Your gifts are so beautiful, but I have gifts, too.

Jennifer: Yep. Like Glinda, from The Wizard Oz, said, "You don't need to be helped anymore. You've always had the power."

Amy: (sighing) that's it.

Jennifer: That's it.

Homework:

Go through each chapter and journal about each lesson and reflect on how the insights you gained from reading have shown up in your own life. What shifts have taken place or have begun to?

Afterword

The topics we introduced here are always expanding and the conversation about how they relate to our lives is always changing. For example, the opening story about Jennifer and "her friend" discussing the moon was actually a reference to the beliefs of AJ, Jennifer's friend, who later died while we were in the middle of writing this book. It was hard to know how to handle that huge change. Do we refocus our book to discuss his passing? Do we write about the emotional toll that losing her friend had on her life? As you can tell, we decided to keep moving forward and we included the lessons that arose in the wake of his departure. Life, death, crazy kids, marital strain, moves, layoffs, and everyday life were happening all around us as we were building this book. We soon realized that none of it was slowing or stopping for our convenience. At times, writing this book felt like trying to maintain a steady pace while walking on a moving floor.

We've had to make some tough choices in this book about how much to share without confusing the message or getting too deep into a particular topic. And then came our personal shifts: Jennifer feeling connected to Catholicism through her conversion and then drifting away from key tenets that no longer spoke to her and Amy's marriage /soul contract work with Brian that helped her see how they have been called together. We were also changing homes, redefining our careers, and processing the dramatic 2016 US Presidential election. Do we include these nuisances or save them for our podcast series, "Spiritual Detox," or maybe for a future book?

The conversations that did end up in the final version of this book will receive varying degrees of support. Some readers will nod and agree with many of the ideas presented, while others will shake their head at the title and refuse to read further.

Receiving mixed reviews for a book, especially one like ours, is not a shocking revelation. You, like this book, contain specific beliefs that may seem controversial to others. Admittedly, you've probably had people in your life who agree or disagree with your views. After reading this book, we hope that you can be detached from someone else's perspective. Your beliefs do not need to be intertwined with the beliefs that someone else holds.

You now know *you* have the power. If nothing else, Divas, please know you have all the power you'll ever need. Knowing that the power resides in you, share your insights with others and then let the attachment go. When you find yourself in a disagreement, give people the courtesy and space to grow and change and shift. Don't demand immediate conversion. Don't expect them to agree with you or even to understand your ideas. Step back and give them independent time to process. Allow for privacy and contemplation; the same amount of space you would want for yourself. When we listen with a love mindset, share with a generous soul, and live without attachment, miracles can happen.

We understand that this isn't always easy. Some days we are working with negativity and we have to be *in* it, to get *through* it. We encourage you to "be in it" when you're feeling negative. Feel those feelings without guilt or shame. Let your mood exist before seeking to banish it. Usually the miracles avoid grouchy days, so there is an advantage to eventually moving on from low simmering rage. When you're ready to be your radiant self again, turn to meditation, fresh air, a detox bath, or a quick outdoor grounding (naked feet on the Earth) to act as a restart button.

Other days we wake up in a state of joy and somehow manage to stay in a space of gratitude despite all the challenges that arise. These are the days when you chuckle at the rude neighbor. You pop open your umbrella without angst during a storm. Things just feel easy and good.

Everyone is different and every day is different, so we'd never want to imply that we all are going to process life's hiccups and tragedies the same way. This book is just one more resource (with a bunch of tools inside) for you to use as you navigate it all. It's all a part of your spiritual growth. And really, what is growth? Answer: It's just a form of stretching that can feel shitty sometimes. If a growth opportunity hurts too much, consider revisiting at a later time. Your timing is not someone else's timing. If you try working on cord-cutting before you're ready, it won't feel empowering or aligned. Another thing: you don't even need to do the homework in the same order that you saw it in the book. We are here to validate it all.

In the end, we want you to know that you can love this book while your brother hates it. That's cool, your brother ain't ready for all this. Plus, it's a book for Divas. Why is he even reading it?

Let your growth and change happen when it's ready. Listen to your inner wisdom and allow the expansion of your awareness to unfold when it feels good. Remember that this book has useful tools that work really well now, but may feel unnecessary later.

It is all a-okay.

Seriously...everything's a-okay and happening *exactly* as it should.

Thanks, Uni!

About the Authors

Amy R Brooks

Amy is the author of *Stuff Your (Super) Mom Forgot to Tell You...* and *Stuff (First-time) Authors Need to Know* and is currently working on a collaborative book project entitled, *Stuff I've Never Told Anyone: Finding Power in the Shadow of Shame.* She is also the founder of VoicePenPurpose Publishing which brings together first-time authors and the resources they need to make their book dreams come true. Amy lives in Maryland with her family.

Jennifer Jiva

Jennifer is a life-long intuitive, an ordained Spiritual Healer- Shamanic Practitioner, and a Reiki Master. She also co-hosts a talk show called "Our Real Talk," works as a Life Mentor for both men and women, and serves as a frequent contributor on various radio programs. Jennifer lives in Iowa with her family.

Want More?

You can learn more about writing your book at
VoicePenPurpose.com. Amy can be reached for
coaching or speaking engagements at
Amy@VoicePenPurpose.com.

Stay connected with Jennifer Jiva and learn
about her upcoming events via
FB: ***Jennifer Jiva-Say It Now*** or by email at
JenniferJiva38@gmail.com.

Additional Resources

Chakras & Crystals

The word **Chakra** comes from the Sanskrit meaning wheel or disc. There are seven major chakras and many minor chakras in our body. Apart from the physical body, each human being has a spiritual body. This spiritual body is composed of vibrations of light (energy) and it envelops the physical body. These chakras are found embedded in our energy field. They resonate at different frequencies corresponding to the colors of the rainbow. These chakras are spinning vortices of energy.

The location of chakras in the energy body corresponds directly to the placement of the endocrine glands in the physical body. Chakras have a direct effect on the state of our physical and emotional health and can impact every aspect of our life, our direction, and our decisions. Their energy body absorbs finer levels of energy from the environment and transmits this through the chakras into the physical body.

The Seven major chakras are:

1. **Root chakra:** This chakra is positioned at the base of the spine, at the top of the legs. This chakra controls our energy levels, our connection to the earth and our ambitions. On a physical level this chakra governs the back, legs, hips, feet, spine and the circulation of blood.

2. **Sacral Chakra:** This chakra is positioned below the navel. It controls your passions, your sexual needs, and the fulfillment of your desires. Physically it controls the sexual organs, bladder, bowel and lower intestine.

3. **Solar Plexus:** The solar plexus controls our will, our personal power. It also controls our upper intestines and upper back and spine. It brings us our strength, our courage and our will to succeed, and achieve and survive.

4. **Heart Chakra:** This chakra is situated in and around the heart area of our physical body. On a physical level it controls the heart and circulation

in the lungs. On a mental level the heart chakra affects our emotions and feeling and how we express them towards ourselves and others.

5. **Throat Chakra:** This chakra is situated in the neck area of the body. On a physical level this chakra governs the throat, thyroid, mouth, teeth, tongue, and jaw. On an emotional level this chakra governs the aspect of communication, will power, truthfulness and creativity.

6. **Third Eye Chakra:** This chakra is situated in the middle of the forehead. On a physical level, this chakra governs the pituitary glands, the skull, eyes, brain and the nervous system. It also governs our senses. On an emotional level this chakra governs knowledge, intuition, and wisdom.

7. **Crown Chakra:** This chakra is situated at the top of the head. Physically this chakra controls the spinal cord brain, and nerves. On a spiritual level this chakra is our connection to the divine healing energy. Miraculous healing and telepathy are both because of this chakra.

8. In a nutshell, when our chakra system is balanced and harmonized, it results in our physical, mental, emotional, and spiritual well-being, thereby allowing us to enjoy perfect health.

Gemstone Qualities

Agate: Balances yin-yang energy, stabilizes the aura. Facilitates discernment. Imparts strength and courage. Opens one to innate creative talents. (Note: There are many forms of agate)

Amethyst: Sedative energy. Facilitates spirituality and contentment. Stone of stability, strength, and peace. Excellent for meditation. Enhances psychic ability.

Citrine: Positive energy- stone needs no cleansing. Dissipates negative energy. Enhances warmth, joy, optimism.

Emerald: Loyalty, sensitivity, harmony, tranquility. Assists in memory retention and mental clarity.

Fluorite: Stability, order, discernment, concentration. Helps one to understand and maintain ideals and the perfection of the Universe.

Jasper: Protection, awareness, insight. Grounding.

Kyanite: Never needs cleaning or clearing, aligns all chakras. Tranquility, communication, psychic awareness.

Excellent for meditation and dream recall.

Lapis Lazuli: Knowledge, wisdom, perfection, protection, and creative expression.

Moonstone: Lunar, female energy, emotional, intuitive, rhythms, cycles, destiny.

Obsidian: Dispels negativity. Grounding, healing, protective. Helps one to clearly see one's flaws and the changes that are necessary. Universal crystal, clarity and consciousness.

Sapphire: Joy, peace, beauty, prosperity.

Selenite: Clarity of consciousness, awareness, insight, good judgment. Aids in accessing past/future lives.

Turquoise: Spiritual attunement, strength, grounding. Protective-excellent for astral travel.

Essential Oils

Cedar wood: Cuts through mental blockages to deepen our connection to spirit. Excellent for deep relaxation, meditation, and psychic work.

Eucalyptus: Psychic cleanser of negative energies, especially from arguments and fights

Frankincense: Helps make one aware that reality is multidimensional; also helps break unwanted ties with the past.

Lavender: Calming, balancing, helps us integrate spirituality into everyday life. Can assist with sleep.

Lemongrass: Stimulates psychic awareness.

Myrrh: Grounds spiritual energy, aids in meditation, helps us move through emotional and spiritual blockages.

Peppermint: Mental stimulant; balances both the overblown and under-developed ego.

Rose: Heart opener, facilitates creativity, helps to bring a spiritual content to sexual relationships.

Sandalwood: Stills the conscious mind so a meditative state can be achieved; helps free the mind from the past.

Tea-Tree: Considered to be a universal cleanser; wide variety of uses.

Tips for Connecting to Intuition

- Be present without judging yourself

- Still your mind the best you can

- Think of as little as possible

- Ask your guides for help

- Become aware of emotions you are having

- Filter out self-talk

- Pay attention to symbols or random things that float in

- Avoid interrupting or second guessing messages

- Trust

Tips for Manifesting

- The #1 thing we can tell you is to be true to your emotions, whatever they are. Good or bad.

- Validate if something is upsetting you get it out but don't put your energy on it so much that it becomes your sole focus

- Manifest from your heart not your ego

- Vision boards are great tools for those who like to "see"

- Singing is a great tool for manifesting! Crank up that song you love and SING while feeling what you WANT!

- Write a letter to your future self-detailing the way your life looks, 6 months from now, a year from now. Whatever feels good for you. Give as much detail as you can, no detail goes unnoticed by the Universe.

- Don't just ask; be open to RECEIVE and BELIEVE you deserve to!

Cord Cutting

It is extremely important before you attempt to energetically cut cords on your own that you are coming from a space and consciousness that has worked through emotional healing that connects you to the deeper experiences and people that are attached. This is not a quick fix energetically, the emotions must be honored.

With that said, when cutting energetic cords, it must never be done from a place of anger or frustration. That just feeds the energy in a negative way between you and the other person. No matter what the circumstances, release the attachment with love. Trust me I know this can be difficult especially in abusive situations. My best advice here is to go back to the soul contracts and look at what you may have needed this experience for in your soul's ultimate growth. You must be open to allowing the space for the other person's energy to show up and be heard.

Do not...I repeat...do not cord cut until this is a place you have reached in your consciousness. If this is not something you feel you can do on your own, please work with a trusted healer and/or energy worker.

As always remember that everyone is different and receive information and energy work differently. Whether you see, feel. hear, or just have a knowing for the exercise it is all right. Relax.

Steps for cord cutting:

- Place yourself in a gentle meditative state and call in your higher-self (pure spiritual self) and the higher-self of the person you are wanting to cut negative cords with.

- Allow the space for both of your highest selves to be present

- Inside of yourself and your energy talk to this person and speak of your connection to them past and present. Allow yourself to start truly digging deep into your emotions; good and bad.

How has your life been affected by this connection? Why are you wanting to cut the negative attachment? Don't stop this communication until you literally feel you have nothing else to say.

- Check what this feels like to you when you speak your truth. Remind yourself and the other that you are both safe.

- Allow the other person to speak of their experience and why they are a part of your journey and vice versa. What have they felt? How has their life been affected? Remember, there is no judgement here. Listen with an open heart from your highest self, ego has no place here. If forgiveness is asked for by this person, remember forgiveness helps you to let go. It doesn't mean you aren't hurt by their choices, but through forgiveness you have the opportunity to free yourselves.

- See, feel, hear, or know where the cord/cords are attached, how big they are, what they look like. Are they all negative? Are there ones that have light? Really check here for the answers.

- If you are someone who wants to visualize using a physical tool such as scissors, a saw, etc. this is the time to decide what you feel would cut through this particular cord. If you are someone who prefers using energy to disintegrate the energy, you will set your intention for that.

- Call in your guides, angels, whatever you feel comfortable and safe calling in to assist you

- Say whatever feels right and true to you about releasing the attachment with love, completing the contract or lesson with this person, etc. Allow them the space to help remove the cord as well. As you go through this process your guides, you, and the other person's energy will be calling in light to replace the negativity that has been feeding the connection.

- Something I have always done is ask Archangel Michael to take the severed cord and transmute it into the light.

- See, feel, or sense where the hole is that was left behind by the cord. Imagine, if you will, what it would look like if you had surgery before they sew you up. Ask that healing and light be sent to that area.

- Take a few comfortable breaths and open your eyes when you are ready.

- Drink plenty of water for the next several hours; re-member it is important to hydrate after any energy work.

Note: We will have an audio healing for cord cutting available for download and purchase on VoicePenPurpose.com